Modernizing Practice Paradigms for New Music

Periodization Theory and Peak Performance Exemplified Through Extended Techniques

THE ART AND SCIENCE OF MUSIC TEACHING AND PERFORMANCE

Series Editor Adina Mornell

Volume Two

PL ACADEMIC RESEARCH

Jennifer Borkowski

Modernizing Practice Paradigms for New Music

Periodization Theory and Peak Performance Exemplified Through
Extended Techniques

PL ACADEMIC RESEARCH

Bibliographic Information published by the Deutsche Nationalbibliothek
The Deutsche Nationalbibliothek lists this publication in the Deutsche
Nationalbibliografie; detailed bibliographic data is available
in the internet at http://dnb.d-nb.de.

Library of Congress Cataloging-in-Publication Data
Names: Borkowski, Jennifer.
Title: Modernizing practice paradigms for new music : periodization theory
    and peak performance exemplified through extended techniques / Jennifer
    Borkowski.
Description: Frankfurt am Main : Peter Lang, 2016. | Series: The art and
    science of music teaching and performance, ISSN 2191-3072 ; v. 2 |
    Includes bibliographical references.
Identifiers: LCCN 2016012807 | ISBN 9783631673973
Subjects: LCSH: Flute--Instruction and study. | Flute--Performance. |
    Music--Performance--Psychological aspects.
Classification: LCC MT340 .B67 2016 | DDC 781.44--dc23 LC record
available at https://lccn.loc.gov/2016012807

Cover and   capdance
Book Design   (www.capdance.com)
                 'For the Eye to Dance is Much Delight'

ISSN 2191-3072
ISBN 978-3-631-67397-3 (Print)
E-ISBN 978-3-653-06720-0 (E-Book)
DOI 10.3726/978-3-653-06720-0
© Peter Lang GmbH
Internationaler Verlag der Wissenschaften
Frankfurt am Main 2016
All rights reserved.
PL Academic Research is an Imprint of Peter Lang GmbH.

Peter Lang – Frankfurt am Main · Bern · Bruxelles · New York ·
Oxford · Warszawa · Wien

This publication has been peer reviewed.

www.peterlang.com

Thanks

Special thanks to the following publishers for the generous permission to use their works:

Hinrichsen Edition, Peters Edition Ltd. London; Bärenreiter-Verlag, Basel; Robert Dick for the use of his work; Zeitvertrieb Wien Berlin and European American Music Distributors Company

Thank you, Andy Icochea and Michael Nicholas for your help with notation.

To the supportive flute community, especially Robert Dick and Helen Bledsoe, who have offered ideas, conversations and friendship over the years, thank you. Thank you, Dieter Flury and Herbert Weissberg for your continued support with my projects and thank you for making Vienna my musical home.

I thank my husband and my children for continued support and encouragement. I have the most supportive 5 and 8 year olds on this earth. It surpasses my dreams to hear, "Mommy, I'm proud of you."

Finally, thank you, Adina Mornell, for initiating me into academic work with such high standards. I am honored to be a part of this series. Your integrity, both academic and personal, sets you apart.

Editor's Preface

The authors who are chosen to publish in the series *The Art and Science of Music Teaching and Performance* address important issues from new perspectives, backed by empirical science. Given that these are innovative answers to questions relevant to an audience of both musicians and researchers, one would ask why anyone would take the time and trouble to go through the publishing process, instead of just posting a PDF online. Aside from the wonderful, physical experience of holding a real book in one's own hands that one misses when using a computer, important social critics and psychologists have also pointed to the consequences of Internet use. In particular, they warn of concentration deficits, cognitive shifts, and the absence of "deep thinking" that may accompany on-screen reading.[1]

To avoid such dangers, authors could also choose to publish their results in article form, submitting their articles to one of the respected and renowned journals of music research that appear both in print and online. Yet, what most prominently sets this book series apart from these other forms of publication is the specific format that allows room for authors to provide insights into the "field use" of their results. It is through the practical application of the learning strategies and training methods presented in these volumes that readers acquire information about how they may expand and enhance music teaching and practice. When theoretical knowledge becomes available in this form, it may aid future generations of musicians in their endeavors.

How and what to practice are two core issues in music pedagogy. Especially when expert performance is the goal of great artists and their teachers. Thus, there could be no better topic for the second volume in this series than Jennifer Borkowski's contemporary approach to mental and physical preparation, practice quality and performance stamina. What began as a dissertation has since evolved into a compendium of interpretative and technical advice with an extensive section of resources on flute repertoire, extended techniques, breathing work, and sport science research on periodization.

---

1 Carr, N. (2010). *The shallows. What the Internet is doing to our brains.* New York: W. W. Norton.

In her work, Borkowski is able to draw on her rich experience as a performer: both on the concert stage and in the ice skating rink. As an orchestra musician, as part of an ensemble, in solo musical performances, and in music lessons, Borkowski has been able to transfer knowledge gained first-hand as a competitive athlete and as a sports coach to the domain of music. It was in the sport sciences that she first encountered the concept of periodization. Her familiarity with both worlds, music and sports, is the foundation on which her work stands.

Throughout her on-going career as a flutist, Borkowski sought out and continues to seek challenges in repertoire. In addition, she is a composer herself. Thus, she both interprets and creates pieces of music that require extended techniques and the use of electronics, "pushing the envelope" of what can be expected from both the instrument and the performer. She has worked with contemporary composers and composer-performers such as Robert Dick, Salvatore Sciarrino and Peter Ablinger. This has given her a chance to receive feedback about notation, sound, and technique directly from the artists themselves – knowledge that this book will pass on to the next generation.

The language of this book may not be typical for an academic publication, as the target audience is wider than the population of musicologists, music and sports psychologists interested in this project. Through discussion, examples, and exercises, this book documents Borkowski's knowledge and understanding of the professional flute literature and of professional performance thereof, in addition to presenting the augmented and revised version of her research. One could see this as a new "composition" that can be expected to become a standard reference work for performers, students, and teachers alike.

One last note on the relevance of this material: This book concerns itself with modern classical music or western art music. As the 20th century began, music composed after the Impressionism and Expressionism periods, was considered Modern, Contemporary or Postmodern. Now, in the 21st century, with the term "modern" already connected with a concrete musical style, and terminologically with nowhere left to go, musical historians have begun to define musical epochs by the calendar, rather than the style. Higher institutions of music such as conservatories and universities have been slow to adapt to new and newer music of the current age. Not only because of this difficulty of nomenclature, but also because newer and newest music is often hard to categorize as belonging to a singular, particular style. As one of Borkowski's empirical studies demonstrates, the standard repertoire for the majority of orchestras is gathered from the 17th to 19th centuries and today's music students have limited to non-existent exposure to music not found in their music textbooks.

In essence then, to go beyond the familiar, a musician must first hear of the existence of a work, then find the score, decipher the notation, and possibly learn different, extended techniques before a discussion of interpretation or aesthetics becomes relevant. It takes curiosity, motivation, and risk to voyage out into the uncharted territory of rarely heard compositions. Comparable to space travel, it is

> [...] the thrust of curiosity that leads men to try to go where no one has gone before.[2]

In keeping with this spirit and as the editor of this series, I welcome the inquisitive reader to view Jennifer Borkowski's *Modernizing Practice Paradigms for New Music* as a musician's guide to a new galaxy of classical music, and hope that you will discover inspiration for the practice of your instrument, for an exploration of the musical pieces discussed here, as well as for your own discovery of works that are yet to be composed as we go to press with this book.

Munich, in January 2016   Adina Mornell

---

2 *Introduction to Outer Space* (1958). Washington, D. C.: U. S. Government Printing Office, p. 1.

List of Figures

List of Tables

I. Introduction

New music is no longer marginalized. Musicians have never been more independent, more diverse and more empowered. The purpose of this book is to further possibilities of growth, modernizing practice paradigms by updating theories of learning and performance preparation. While creating new learning models, I use information from fields that have studied stamina, peak performance and practice efficiency – scientifically. Modern repertoire includes new and extended playing techniques, but musicians are still studying in the same ways we always have.

To date, pedagogical materials have given us dictionaries of extended techniques and composers have developed a grammar in using them. In just the past few years, new technology has created tremendous ease of access to these materials. For example, as an offshoot of Robert Dick's ground-breaking work in developing new fingerings, Andrew Botros developed an algorithm which notates all of the possible fingerings for multiphonics, microtones and altered timbres. Now a flutist or composer can bring a phone or tablet into a practice room and access every mathematical fingering possibility. YouTube has changed accessibility to new music. Everyone can now hear repertoire that was previously only heard in new music festivals. Extended techniques used to be a mystery, requiring a brute strength and score reading prowess to figure them out. Now we have expert models of them online. Robert Dick, Helen Bledsoe and Matthias Ziegler, among others, have made excellent online tutorials. One YouTube channel syncs recordings of Brian Ferneyhough's works with the score. In addition to this, new music has had some very public successes. In 2012, Claire Chase was awarded a MacArthur Fellowship for her work with I.C.E. (International Contemporary Ensemble). Greg Patillo, the beat boxing flutist, composed a piece for the National High School Soloist's Competition for the National Flute Association. Selected conservatories have added programs in contemporary performance practice and new faculty are increasingly reflecting our stylistic diversity.

In spite of these successes, there is still a divide among musicians. Resistance to learning music composed since World War II remains. Opinions expressing resistance or dislike are easy to find. James Pappoutsakis, former principal flutist of the Boston Symphony, has remarked, "Contemporary music should not distort the tone quality or degrade the player."[3] This reflects the idea that classical musicians strive for a homogenous tone, and that when we step outside of this, we're wrong. The composer Virgil Thompson said, "The European effort toward writing atonal music not for noise-making instruments but for those whose design has been perfected over centuries for avoiding tonal obfuscation has been [....] a waste of effort, save possible for proving it could be done."[4]

Besides these opinions among mainstream musicians, academia has its own biases. Robert P. Morgan, in his textbook *Twentieth Century Music; A History of Musical Style in Modern Europe and America*, dedicates only two paragraphs to the importance of IRCAM, Institut de Recherche et Coordination Acoustique/Musique, and makes only a brief mention of the Darmstadt Ferienkurse.[5] The name is written only in passing, omitting any discussion of its philosophy or current influence on composition.

The editors of *Source* magazine had the following comment:

> Since, by definition, the avant-garde is at the 'growing edge' of music, new scores must be published and circulated while their concepts are fresh, not years after the composition. [...] In this way, everyone gains true perspective, and music advances. [...] While it is a fact that not everyone - least of all professional musicians and educators - *wants* to make an effort to gain 'true perspective,' it is equally true that new music will advance and eventually take over the most conservative citadels of learning - for the simple reason that it always has, always does, and always will do so.[6]

There is still a stylistic divide. In 2007, I conducted a randomized study and saw this more clearly. The study was carried out through the "Flute List Pages," a listserv with over 2000 members. 187 flutists agreed to participate in a blind study with the requirement that they were teaching or majoring in music in an American university music program. There were no qualifiers for majors, meaning this was a randomized selection including graduates

3 Toff (1985) p. 280.
4 Thompson (1981) p. 11.
5 Both IRCAM and Darmstadt were profoundly influenced by Pierre Boulez as he wanted to move music in new directions after World War II. Darmstadt was founded in 1946 by Wolfgang Steineke, and various composers who took part there were Pierre Boulez, Luigi Nono, György Ligeti, Karlheinz Stockhausen, John Cage, Luciano Berio and many others. IRCAM, was founded in 1969 by Pierre Boulez and was funded by the French Government and Georges Pompidou. Boulez served as director of IRCAM from 1970 until 1992.
6 Chase (1967) p. 80.

and undergraduates in both music performance and music education. The following data proved noteworthy:

Table 1: Survey Responses

Extended Technique Experience	85
No Experience	102
Age Range	18-39

(n=187)

From these flutists, 85 had studied at least one work with extended techniques. From those 85, the response was overwhelmingly positive towards new music in general. Many were rock/jazz based with two classical students having credited *Jethro Tull* with their exposure to new techniques. What was missing from 100% of the flutists was any advanced work or work of the *new complexity*.[7] Also, appearing only once was Luciano Berio's *Sequenza I* (1958), and no one had played any work of Pierre Boulez.

Because of the speed at which technology is changing our access, and because of the recent and very public successes of Claire Chase and Greg Patillo, I am going to suggest two things. One, by the time I correlated the answers from the respondents in this study and secured this publishing contract, these answers might no longer reflect the current situation. Two, with ease of accessibility to extended techniques tutorials, and with young, energetic role models like Chase and Patillo, there is no longer any excuse not to learn them. The stigma of being misunderstood by making "noises" is no longer valid.

During the study mentioned above, some respondents who do not teach modern repertoire said that it was not needed for their students' careers. Others said that their students were not ready. One said that she does not see that her students will need new music, as they are majoring in music education. Harry Partch in his *Genesis of a Music* (1947) writes about this very idea, that of education:

---

7 New complexity is a compositional movement dating from approximately 1970. Compositions are known for using dense notation incorporating poly-rhythms, extended techniques and microtonality thus making the scores highly demanding and sometimes unplayable for the performer.

> It is not difficult for the alert student to acquire the traditional techniques. Under the pressures of study these are unconsciously and all too easily absorbed. The extent to which an individual can resist being blindly led by tradition is a good measure of his vitality.[8]

Partch calls it *unconscious*. Will extended techniques become unconscious as well? Music students spend hours practicing in small practice rooms adjacent to one another. A common aesthetic penetrates the walls. Partch talks about the desire musicians have to improve, and that this definition of improvement is too narrow. He criticizes musicians for wanting to improve only performance skills. He continues that "good pianists, good teachers, good composers, and 'good' music no more creates a spirit of investigation and a vital age in music than good grades in school create a spirit of investigation and a body of thinking citizens."[9] In the current changing arts economy, musicians would be wise to create a new vital age in music.

We're in a different place historically with new music. It used to be that the performers who took on a new work had to decipher it on their own, learning new notations, new techniques and internalizing the sound language of a composer. This process shows tremendous respect for a musical work. It speaks to the dedication and time-consuming process of realizing a composer's imagination. Nonetheless, performers who had gone through that process came through changed. This changed their listening, their musicality and their concept of their role as an interpreter of new music. This intense relationship, the relationship between performer and work, creates a palpable energy in a performance. I believe, personally, that this energy was what I was drawn to when I was first exposed to new music. Now we are in a time where we can simply imitate the forerunners. The new sound world is accessible for all of us. This might mean that new music gets new ideas. It might also mean that this working process dissipates.

Aims

In order for new music to keep its fire and its intense work ethic, I am suggesting that we need to modernize ideas of practice and peak performance. There is a process of self-discovery that happens when one enters into a new sound language and takes the responsibility for its realization. This book identifies elements in that process and gives them a structure.

8 Partch (1947).
9 Ibid.

Research in sports science has shown success with maximizing performance capabilities while minimizing the risks of overuse injuries. These successes will be analyzed and then adapted for a musical context. New music requires both an intellectual or logical involvement and an increased body awareness or physicality. Much new music requires more stamina than traditional repertoire.

This is taught through two main concepts: the broader concept of practice variability and the more focused training of periodization. The two go hand in hand. Practice variability ensures maximal learning with minimal repetition and periodization creates peak performances. By varying tasks, both the logical and physical work can be attended to. Periodization teaches the performer about energy expenditure and builds endurance with embouchure, breathing and concentration.

The application of periodization is taught first by creating a continuum of extended techniques, focusing on each technique in isolation and then by applying periodization in a sample program leading to a performance of *(t)air(e)* (1980-83) for solo flute by Heinz Holliger.

Changing practice paradigms extends to any instrument and every repertoire. This is vital in all fields of music, in all levels of music education and for live concerts to succeed. This ensures that we don't become merely imitators of sound, but thoughtful interpreters. Modernizing ideas of practice and preparation addresses our willingness to step out of the confines of our techniques, even when those techniques are already "extended."

II. Motivation for the Unconvinced

a. Using Extended Techniques to Diagnose and Reframe Technical Issues

This section addresses some of the questionnaire respondents' informal answers as to why they didn't play new music. Several said that they were not ready and cited specific problems with embouchure. I subsequently wrote exercises for them using extended techniques to solve their technical problems.

Extended techniques can be used as strengthening exercises. They can reframe practice for a student who has been fruitlessly trying something over and over again. There is no limit as to when they can begin. While many techniques take more energy, not all require the refined embouchure control of traditional playing.[10] In fact, non-flutists could learn some of the techniques more quickly than they could learn to play a classical flute tone. There is a tendency to assign all extended techniques to a category as more difficult than traditional ones.[11] However, what makes them "extended" is not necessarily their difficulty level, but that in a historical sense, they extend the tonal color palette.

The following problems will be discussed and solutions with extended techniques will be offered:

1. Shyness

Sometimes shy students have a refined musical sense and are carefully working at making the flute sound very pretty. What they don't yet realize is that breaking them out of their box will open their sound making it even more resonant. For students who are naturally shy, working with the diaphragm can open them up and eventually their sound as well. Jet whistle is the most accessible example. Students can be taught to blow a lot of air without focusing on the resulting tone. Done as a quick warm-up, jet whistle gets the diaphragm moving and wakes up the body. The teacher can guide the student into using more and more air each time until the diaphragm is push-

10 The exceptions here are whistle tones, multiphonics and harmonics.
11 http://www.fluteworld.com/index.php?action=strona&wart=16, Retrieved December 10, 2012.

ing as hard as it can. The emphasis is just on making noise; therefore, the student should not feel inhibited about making wrong or ugly sounds. After the jet whistle is learned, experimentation can be done by adding fingers, rolling the head joint either in or out, changing the mouth position or with consecutive jet whistles.

The second technique that can be used for an inactive diaphragm is tongue-ram. The tongue ram will not sound at an acceptable volume level if the diaphragm does not give a real punch. It can be practiced by playing one note at a time, then by progressing to consecutive tones and then finally a full scale. When playing duets, the student will hear how much more diaphragm motion they need in order to match the volume of a normal flute tone. This added energy level is only beneficial when returning to traditional repertoire.[12]

2. Weak Articulation

Tongue pizzicato can be taught to students who tongue poorly. Sometimes a student will not use the tip of the tongue, fearing that it sounds too harsh. Tongue pizzicato requires a quick and explosive motion of the tongue which can show variances of pressure and speed that the tongue can make. Another benefit for the teacher is that both tongue pizzicato and tongue ram can be practiced without the flute, making the tongue visible. A teacher can solve many problems by showing the student differences with the speed of the tongue in a mirror.

3. Tight Embouchure

For loosening a "tight" or "smiling" embouchure, multiphonics can help. Because both tones cannot be reached with a tight embouchure, the flutist must learn to relax the lips, almost like a pure beginner without a refined embouchure, in order to accommodate both tones.

Also useful in loosening up tight lips are air sounds. For a student with an extremely tight or *biting* embouchure, experimenting with air sounds can challenge the belief that the tone must be extremely focused in order to project. The problem with a biting embouchure is that the tone does not have

12 A recommendation for repertoire teaching this is in *Flute Talk* magazine: Borkowski, J., December 2010, "Repertoire with extended techniques for all ages."

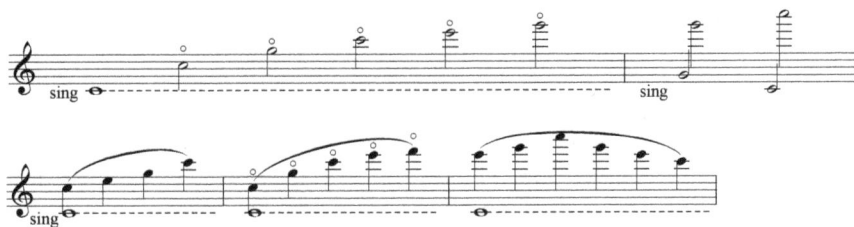

Figure 1d: Developing a quiet third octave

Figure 1e: Smiling or tight embouchure

Figure 1f: Smiling or tight embouchure

Figure 1g: Weak tonguing

Figure 1h: Weak tonguing

Concluding Remarks

Often, a student with a problem is not able to hear it. Putting it into a different context can open up the ear. In addition to this, when breaking students out of a learning plateau, practice variability is a recommended teaching technique.[13] Trust that these techniques open up new body awareness and promote greater energy when returning to traditional repertoire. This practical, problem solving application of extended techniques makes for a positive first exposure.

b. Using Extended Techniques to Promote Flow

In one of the informal responses from the questionnaire respondents, a student told me that she loved playing *Density 21.5*, but was afraid that the audience wouldn't get it. I suppose she is not alone in feeling this way. After what we have read about prejudices against new music and from the discussions we hear from our colleagues, we usually know whom we are performing for. New music can be a marginalized music and some of its greatest critics remark that it is only for academics, and that it is a closed, self-serving circle. We have new notations to learn, new fingering systems and new embouchure demands. It can be very easy to dismiss new music when you feel that all of your effort will land on an unappreciative audience.

There is a second case to be made for learning new music. Not just that it is good for technique, but that it is good for learning in general. When we look back at our original needs for music and what music brought us when we were younger, we find that music satisfies our need for play.

Piaget sees play as essential for learning[14] and music satisfies these needs. These are three types of play and their musical applications:

- **Play with practice**

  What are the possibilities of my instrument?

13 Davids, Bennett, Newell (2006) p. 112.
14 Altman (1986) pp. 10 -12.

- **Play with symbols and characters**

  What can I imitate on my instrument? Can I engage in As/If play, leading to greater expression?

- **Play with rules**

  What new rules are here for me to understand and master?

New music reopens these avenues of self-discovery after we have become comfortable with traditional repertoire. There is a point in every musician's development when he hits a learning plateau. Reintroducing play through new music is in agreement with psychologists' recommendations for bringing a student out of a plateau, and that is, to introduce new ways of practicing. The previous chapter on using extended techniques to reframe other problems was an example of that. New repertoire, new techniques, new notations and new scores are a prime example of playing with rules. This is puzzle solving. This frees up our ideas of practice being merely for a performance. Practice becomes process once more. It is good for us as people and for our own development.

In a chapter in the book *The Body is the Message* (2012), I discuss using extended techniques as stress inoculation and the concept of flow, coined by Csikszentmilhalyi (1992). A flow states promotes

> [...] focused concentration, a sense of outcomes under the person's own control, a distorted sense of time (e.g. an hour of practice seems to go by quickly), losing a sense of self-awareness, and experiencing the activity as intrinsically rewarding.[15]

Further,

> [...] to remain in flow, the complexity of the activity must increase by developing new skills and taking on new challenges.[16]

Composers of the new complexity can consider themselves vindicated. Younger composers who are criticized for imitating the new complexity can also consider themselves empowered. There is a purpose for this. Even if this music is just for us, it is good for us to learn. At some point, we can disregard any criticisms of new music as we accept that it brings about positive changes in us. We develop physically and we are challenged creatively.

15 Borkowski (2012) p. 35.
16 O'Neill and McPherson (2002) p. 35.

Peter Röbke pinpoints this when he says:

> The central pedagogical question is: What expressive areas are opened to me by works of the twentieth century? [...] because when I clear these things in a piece, I strengthen myself; how deeply I sink myself into a composition, I sink into and differentiate my ability to be expressive.[17]

Thus, new music can be seen not only for its artistic worth, but also for its pedagogical value. As new music inherently stretches boundaries in composition, it also stretches boundaries in teaching, learning, and practice.

17 Röbke (2000) p. 144, Original German text: "Die zentrale didaktische Frage lautet im folgenden: Welche Ausdrucksmöglichkeiten eröffnen mir Werke des 20. Jahrhunderts? [...] denn indem ich die Sache kläre, stärke ich mich selbst; indem ich mich in die Kompositionen vertiefe, vertiefe und differenziere ich meine Ausdrucksfähigkeit." Translation by Jennifer Borkowski.

III. A Work Ethic Against Mediocrity

The effort that is required to grasp new music is not one of abstract knowledge, nor is it the acquaintance with some system or other, with theorems, much less with mathematical procedures. It is essentially imagination, what Kierkegaard called the speculative ear.[18]

Søren Kierkegaard's reference is made about dualities of emotion. Music, however, need not remain in mere dualities. In order to perform Brian Ferneyhough's music, one does indeed require knowledge of mathematical procedures. Ferneyhough remarks that music "is not based on an exclusive 'either-or' but a 'both-and.'"[19] The speculative ear, however, is a vivid idea that speaks to how we listen. We can differentiate between how we listen, how we actively interpret a piece of music that we intend to perform and how we coax an audience to listen. Must listeners comprehend music before it is appreciated? Comprehension is an act of the mind. Appreciation takes place when the listener is personally engaged.

New music's circle is notoriously small. We tend to think that new music is for the intellectual musician only. However,

Adorno asserts that to grasp modern music what is needed is essentially fantasy [...] He points out the ways in which [...] subjective capacity that would enable individuals to grasp modern music, i.e. the speculative ear and appropriate ways of paying attention or concentrating, are made difficult by that society's life conditions.[20]

Now we are even more distracted than when Adorno was still living. In contrast to the bombardment of advertisements and 24 hour news cycles, I feel relieved that music does not tell me what to think, but gives me something to think about. There aren't clear dividing lines between listening and performing either, because while we are performing we are indeed listeners as well, overhearing and shaping our own performance. We balance imagination and logic.

The speculative ear can grasp a new sound language. The speculative ear can hear music that it doesn't yet know how to listen to. This type of con-

18 Adorno (2002) p. 674.
19 Ferneyhough (1998) p. 391.
20 Shapiro (2005).

centration, or thoughtful immersion, is also another type of hearing. Helmut Lachenmann (*Musik als existentielle Erfahrung*, Music as an Existential Experience) has revised his ideas on hearing over the years. The essay that was, 'hearing is worthless without thinking' evolved into 'hearing is worthless without feeling.' In the end, he called it, 'hearing is worthless without hearing'[21] and clarified

> Hearing is something different than listening to understand content. It is, hearing differently, to discover within oneself new antennae, new sensory information and new sensibilities. It also means to discover your own changeability.[22]

If we are going to discover changeability within ourselves and have any hope of coaxing a speculative ear out of our listeners, we need a new an adapted work ethic. Pierre Boulez said that

> [...] the student wanting to enter the contemporary field must [...] jump with a miniature parachute, taking his life in his hands. How many are brave enough to make that jump?[23]

While ease of access to learning materials may have negated some of this, there is an evolved truth in this idea. New music has been performed by the most committed among us. Brute strength was necessary to tackle new scores. New teaching materials and greater dissemination of recordings now make this learning process easier. However, in order to keep mediocrity at bay, one must still feel equally as strongly. It might not be the jump into an unknown notation or technique, but a jump into a deepened relationship among the self, the possibilities of the instrument and the mind of the composer. It may be a willingness to wrestle an aesthetic until it is understood. The commitment and engagement must be palpable.

21 Lachenmann (2004) p. 117. Original German text: Vor vierzehn Jahren, 1971, beim Stuttgart Theorienkongress, zur Zeit der Studentenunruhen, hieß ich meine These: „Hören ist wehrlos ohne Denken." 1978, sieben Jahre später, knüpfte ich daran und ergänzte: Hören ist wehrlos ohne Fühlen" und versuchte durch diese Beschreibung der Bedingungen des Hörens Denken und Fühlen als einander bedingend zu präzisieren. Heute, nach weiteren sieben Jahren, ist mein Vertrauen in die Sprache angeschlagen – auch sie ist oft selbst im Weg, und so sage ich jetzt nur noch: „Hören ist wehrlos – ohne Hören."
22 Ibid. p. 117, Original text: „Denn solche Form des wahrnehmenden Hörens bietet sich nicht unbefangen an, sie muss erst freigelegt werden. Freilegen aber heißt, Dazwischenliegendes wegräumen, jene in der Gesellschaft vorgegebenen dominierenden Hörgewohnheiten, Hörkategorien außer Kraft setzen, aussperren. Hören ist schließlich etwas anderes als verständnisinniges Zuhören, es meint: anders hören, in sich neue Antennen, neue Sensorien, neue Sensibilitäten entdecken, heißt also auch, seine eigene Veränderbarkeit entdecken und sie der so erst bewusst machen." Translation by the author.
23 http://www.helenbledsoe.com, Retrieved February 14, 2013.

Brian Ferneyhough in *Shattering the Vessels of Received Wisdom* says:

> One encounters two types of performer; one that might be termed the 'gig' musician – the player who, in a couple of rehearsals, is justly proud of producing a 'professional' realization of just about anything. Often, such individuals are required to interpret vastly different styles in close juxtaposition and have, in consequence, developed a technique of rapid reading and standardized, averaged-out presentation in order to maximize effectivity, [...] what happens is that whole chunks of conventional wisdom in terms of musical *thinking* are also absorbed.[24]

Going back to Harry Partch's comments in the introduction, musical style is *unconsciously* absorbed. I believe that new music's edge is that the interpretive process is conscious. It has, built into its complexity, the necessity to slow down and learn the score and go to depths not necessary in works that can be sight-read. In *Unity Capsule*, Ferneyhough writes that his work "demands much of the serious interpreter by way of self-analysis on both conscious and body-conscious levels."[25] Now, in addition to balancing logic and imagination, we balance consciousness with body-awareness. When talking about *Cassandra's Dream Song* he says that the "logical sections are intended to sensibilize the flutist to the nuances of energy-expenditure."[26] We oscillate between conscious and body-conscious. We learn about the upper ends of energy-expenditure, both through physical energy and intense concentration.

Ferneyhough's differentiation, conscious and body-conscious, mirrors methodology I had learned years ago while studying sports science. The following sections introduce periodization and practice variability to developing both conscious and body-conscious skill, along with the necessary training for managing energy expenditure. Using ease of access to new learning materials as a springboard, I've taken the intense working process of learning new works and given this process a formal structure.

24 Ferneyhough, op. cit., (1993) p. 393.
25 Ibid. p. 369.
26 Ibid. p. 378.

IV. Mental Preparation – Conscious Preparation

a. Reading and Listening

Because of the diversity of new works and the need to learn a new sound language, conscious preparation means learning the composer's language and style. Concrete listening assignments can lessen the guilt about the time away from the practice room. This is the first paradigm shift in moderniz-ing practice routines; preparation includes more time away from the instru-ment. There is musical maturity and stylistic understanding to develop. For example, a student focusing intently on learning a Mozart concerto might not find the humor and lightness as readily as a student who is also familiar with his comedic operas. New music is not any different. Understanding the composer's mind through multiple works and texts facilitates cohesive interpretations. Listening should be done critically, however. A quick listen "to see how it goes" doesn't move us further down the path towards musical autonomy.

Since there is comparatively little formal coursework in new music, read-ing assignments are also important. A student should take the initiative to identify the compositional school and corresponding philosophy that the composer belongs to. Music theory and aesthetics since 1945 are largely based on philosophical texts.

Personally speaking, I found Brian Ferneyhough first accessible through writ-ten texts. I felt that I understood his thought process before I understood his music. The essays from which I have already quoted have been paramount in shaping my work. Beyond my formal work, these essays gave new music both depth and clarity that has engaged my own thought process. After his texts grabbed my attention, I was then drawn towards his music.

The intention of this recommendation is not to lay out a step-by-step teaching plan, or a comprehensive reading list. However, by way of example, the ar-ticle *Cassandra's Dream Song: A Literary Feminist Perspective* can empower a flutist to tackle this piece whereas the notes on the page, and perhaps recordings as well, might immediately dissuade. The abstract reads:

> Brian Ferneyhough's solo flute music 'Cassandra's Dream Song' can be interpreted in the light of Christa Wolf's book 'Cassandra.' The novel concerns the develop-

ment of a woman's whole character. Similarly, a musician can consider a performance as an expression of individuality, in collaboration with the composer. The flute music is thus seen as an attempt by Cassandra to find her own voice in a man's world.[27]

The Cassandra myth is bigger than even this one example. However, this exemplifies the work ethic I am talking about. Ellen Waterman took the time not only to read about Ferneyhough, but to read a novel as well. From there, she created her own interpretation of the piece. Having a purpose beyond winning a competition is invaluable. While in pursuit of an artistic goal, *purpose* is a force that energizes the work process.

Concluding Thoughts

Overall, the musician taking the responsibility for this research will be better served than either the musician given sound bites of information by a teacher, or the musician who imitates recordings or performances of colleagues. Conscious preparation creates interpretations that are both informed and personal. The relationship between composer and performer deepens. One then becomes an autonomous interpreter of new music.

b. Notation

It is often after the first glance at the music that a decision is made to play or not play a particular piece. Modern notation can be very offsetting with its unfamiliar symbols, handwritten scores, rhythms and unrecognizable time signatures. When selecting works for a performance, it is helpful to make a distinction between those works that use experimental notation and those that need to be realized quickly. While composers are often trying to experiment with sound via new notations, ideally, there would be a place for performers to decipher them when they have fewer time constraints. However, interpreters are often pushed to learn many new pieces very quickly, and to perform them within days of receiving the score.

In the same vein as reading about the composer's sound language and ideas, interpreting notation is another piece of conscious preparation. Misunderstanding or confusion is not the same as a creative license. One must be diligent in interpreting exactly what is called for. For example, while a

27 Waterman, (1994) p. 154.

student may hear the rhythm as being "free," an experienced teacher will simply hear lack of control. This aural development takes time, and one must remember this when interpreting new music.

To develop receptiveness to new notation, understanding the composer's purpose is helpful. Ross Lee Finney states that composition

> [...] has never been quite satisfactory for the composer's purposes and therefore the experiment continues. Why is this process frowned upon? Musical notation is one of the most amazing picture languages of the human animal. It didn't come into being of a moment but is the result of centuries of experimentation.[28]

Interpreting notation is another skill area to be nurtured. Just as one develops the skill of sight-reading, quickness and flexibility with new notations will be developed over time. A new music interpreter must adjust to the continual development of notation.

The common use and accessibility of composition software such as *Sibelius* and *Finale* have helped composers use standard notation models. However, even when composers adhere to these suggestions, many new effects have not yet been replicated by either other composers or software and need new symbols. The following is a short discussion meant to illuminate some of the countless situations interpreters face with various notation schemes. Perhaps these examples will raise more questions than they answer. That is the point to be made. This is an element of new music that performers must continually analyze and question; and, this is the part of the work of interpreting a score.

The examples from flute literature are as follows:
- Fingering systems
- Head joint position and embouchure position

Fingering Systems

The clearest fingering charts to read are Robert Dick's. The flutist reads his music as a musical score with the fingerings directly beneath each tone. They are pictorial, mirroring the flute keys. The flutist needs only to depress the blackened keys and lift the empty keys. The only pedagogical difficulty

28 Cage, (1969) without page numbers.

with this is that the flutist can spend more time reading the fingerings and not the resulting tones. Nonetheless, this is a very accessible way to introduce new fingerings.

Figure 2: Robert Dick, *Flying Lessons, Volume 1, number 1*. Reprinted with the kind permission of Robert Dick

Bernhard Lang in *Schrift I* uses a numbering system of a pianist, with the fingers numbered one through five beginning with the thumbs. This is helpful if you're a pianist; confusing if you're a flutist. The left hand position is reversed and the flute has one non-active thumb, making the first active finger, finger number two.

Figure 3: Bernhard Lang, *Schrift I*, measure 135. Reprinted with the kind permission of Zeitvertrieb Wien Berlin

Tōru Takemitsu in *Voice* uses a notation for fingerings without a key explanation. The explanation for his fingering graph is as follows:

The holes of the flute are shown graphically as the left and right hands. The auxiliary keys of the flute are numbered from top to bottom. This means that the left hand thumb is an auxiliary key and is number one. Two is the left hand pinky. Keys three, four and five are, from left to right, the Bb lever and the two trill keys. Six through nine are the pinky keys on the foot joint, beginning with the Eb key, progressing down to C#, C natural, and low B.

Another approach is in Klaus Huber's *Ein Hauch von Unzeit* or in Salvatore Sciarrino's *L'opera per Flauto*. Fingerings for pitch sets are provided in the glossary. It is time consuming to flip back and forth from the fingering chart to the corresponding tones, but in time, the fingerings are learned. During the learning process, similarities in fingerings are learned and this approach prompts the flutist to memorize the fingerings.

As a pedagogical problem, one clearly sees that the lack of uniformity is the first challenge. A flutist must first decipher the performance notes before sight-reading is possible. Composers use various fingering systems that the flutist must experiment with to see which tones are sounding. One cannot simply trust the fingerings and follow them. Another solution is to simply omit or ignore them. Georg Friedrich Haas has omitted fingerings in his *Finale* for solo flute. It is highly microtonal and one must memorize, or pencil in, the fingerings that work. In actuality, this isn't any more work than solving the problems of the other systems. First, there is a size benefit; the music fits on the stand. Second, other fingering systems do not account for the variances among flutes. Closed holes, B feet and split E keys will alter some pitches and the flutist must critically use a fingering guide (Botros, Dick, Levine,) as a comparison. Individual preferences regarding embouchure and head joint models also play a large role in deciding on the fingering. After all, altered fingerings mean altered color.

Head Joint Position and Embouchure Position

The important work for the interpreter here is deciding what is either a color effect, a recommendation for achieving the proper pitch or choreography. Answers are not always clear.

In *Schrift I* by Bernhard Lang, measure 6 uses a graphic symbol of Robert Dick depicting an outwardly turned head joint. Robert Dick intended this symbol to yield various pitches with different head joint angles, as seen here:

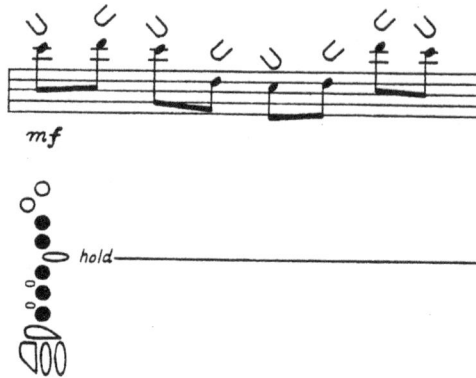

Figure 4: Robert Dick, *Flying Lessons Volume I*, page 22. Reprinted with the kind permission of Robert Dick

In this example, the tones A and the B are not reachable with the same embouchure. Turning the head joint outwards allows for the major second that one cannot reach with a normal playing position. Bernhard Lang uses the same symbol, referencing Robert Dick in the *"Zeichenerklärungen"* (Explanation of Symbols), but uses it for a different function. Isolating each effect in measure six, one sees the following:

Figure 5: Bernhard Lang, *Schrift I*, measure 6. Reprinted with the kind permission of Zeitvertrieb Wien Berlin

The top line of the score shows a widening embouchure that would make the tone breathier and less focused. This leaves one wondering what the difference is between this airy sound and the *aeolischer klang* found in measures one through five. The second line asks that head joint be turned outwards, but does not show any change of pitch. This raises the question of whether there should be a rise in pitch or not, and if not, if one is permitted to alter the pitch. The third line asks for the diaphragm to be used, presumably to achieve the graphically notated vibrato in line four, at a piano dynamic. All put together, in three beats at a speed of 184 beats per minute, produces the equivalent of an air sound with vibrato along with a visual effect of the flute turning outwards.

Beat Furrer's *auf tönernen füssen* asks for an embouchure that is opened to the side. Flutists often release to the side in order to taper notes without any extra air sound. Beat Furrer, however, asks for the mouth to be opened to the side to presumably produce an air sound. The score does not specifically call for that, but it is not notated *ordinario* as other sections are and one is coming from a position of having the mouthpiece completely covered. One must assume then that this is meant to produce a sound in progression from a closed mouthpiece. Also, covering the mouthpiece lowers the pitch of the flute by major 7th. Opening the mouth to the side would raise the sounding pitch.

*)Mund seitlich öffnen

Figure 6: Beat Furrer, *auf tönernen füssen*, page 2, line 1 © by Bärenreiter Verlag, Basel. Used by kind permission

When there are discrepancies, the musician has some decision making to do. Do you produce the proper pitch, ignoring headjoint position or do you perform the prescribed headjoint position while allowing changes in pitch?

The process of decoupling parameters of notation makes each element conscious to the performer. In some cases, the decoupling brings such consciousness to the moment that perhaps this was the intended effect, more so than the replication of written pitches. Rather than learn in a hierarchical way, first rhythm and pitch, then color and expression, the performer is conscious not only of what sounds but also what shows. Conflict need not be dissuasive. In my conversations with flutists during the survey mentioned in the introduction, some said they hate new music because composers don't know what they are doing. At first glance, this may appear to be the case. Looking further, there are performance lessons to be learned by tackling a notation where decoupling causes conflict.

The pedagogical issue isn't really whether notation is clear or not, but how much time the performer has before a performance, and what lessons are learned through learning a new system.

Some notations are both experimental and clear. Toshio Hosokawa, in *Vertical Song I* (1995), devised notation to show three distinct grades of breathiness.

This corresponding graded system is also used in the piece to show the length of fermatas, with the square fermatas being the most extreme. This notation, while requiring a visual adjustment, allows the flutist to follow a logical system of gradation. It is instructive as well. Hosokawa composes in an experimental way, but with a system that can be quickly understood.

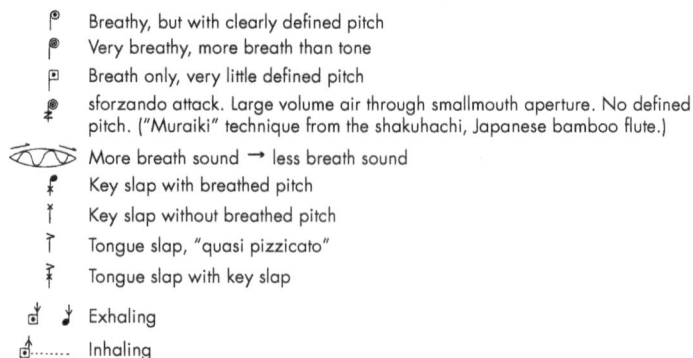

Breathy, but with clearly defined pitch
Very breathy, more breath than tone
Breath only, very little defined pitch
sforzando attack. Large volume air through smallmouth aperture. No defined pitch. ("Muraiki" technique from the shakuhachi, Japanese bamboo flute.)
More breath sound → less breath sound
Key slap with breathed pitch
Key slap without breathed pitch
Tongue slap, "quasi pizzicato"
Tongue slap with key slap
Exhaling
Inhaling

Figure 7: Toshio Hosokawa, *Vertical Song I* © 1995 by Schott Music, Co. Tokyo. All rights reseved. Used by permission of European American Music Distrbuters Company, sole U.S. and Canadian agent for Schott Music Co. Ltd., Tokyo

Bernhard Lang, on the other hand, composes in an experimental way but with a different purpose. In *Schrift I, he* quotes Pierre-Yves Artaud in the use of "aeolischer klang", or air sounds.[29] This symbol is difficult to read because it resembles a percussive symbol similar to key clicks and pizzicato. The visual effect is not one that portrays openness. One wouldn't naturally think to keep the mouth relaxed and open while looking at a downward pointing arrow. Does this matter? Is Lang looking to make a score easily readable, or to create a relationship between the score and the performer? It is called "Schrift," German for handwriting. It is indeed handwritten. He is dialoguing with us in a way that causes questioning, self-reflection and criticism. His music is a handwritten letter, and by writing it this way, he ensures that his work either gets proper time or is not played.

Notation is instructive. When we look further into a notation's message, and withhold judgment of good or bad, notation is another vehicle to deepen the relationship between composer and performer.

c. Microtonality

New music is known for its use of microtonality. There is a marked difference in pieces requiring exact microtonal pitches and those that supply fingerings of non-exact microtonal sequences. The former requires a highly developed ear for proper tuning while the latter only requires a fingering adjustment.[30]

The use of alternate tunings in non-Western music is a discussion worthy of another book. However, looking only at Western music, the history of microtonality is shockingly long. Before the invention of equal temperament, tuning was often a hot and debated topic. After equal temperament came into the picture, the next logical step was to divide the twelve-step octave once more into 24 equal parts, or quartertones.

As early as 1920, Czech composer Alois Hába wrote his *String Quartet, No. 2, Op. 7* using quartertones. The development of microtonality on the flute begins with the equally measured quartertone scale, that is, tones that are 50 cents apart. The first microtonal work for the Boehm system flute is

---

29 Found in the „Zeichenerklärungen" of *Schrift I.*
30 Among the questionnaire respondents who had played contemporary pieces, the vast majority had played pieces that were written with microtonal components, not true quarter-tones. For example, pitches are notated as „somewhat higher."

from 1973: Bruno Bartolozzi's *New Sound for Woodwind* which includes the *Metodo per Flauto* by Pier Luigi Mencarelli. Although known among many composers, this method is hardly known among flutists.[31] In it, the first quartertone fingerings and exercises for the Boehm system flute are found. He writes exercises based on traditional intervals, beginning from a major second through a major seventh. This accomplishes the task of developing intonation. The flutist can tune the familiar interval while transposing it up a quartertone. He then writes short phrases presenting quarter tones in a more modern musical context.

Robert Dick has used sheer experimentation to produce *The Other Flute* in 1989. He has notated two quartertone scales, one for both open and closed-hole flutes. The scales range from D1 to E3. In addition to that, he notated the tendency of the tones under each fingering. That is, too high or low, loud or soft, bright or edgy. In addition to the scales, he also founded tones up to a sixteenth of a tone. He chose the fingerings not for the intonation possibilities but rather for the constancy of the tone color.

In certain microtonal segments one can use chromatic fingerings where one key is left open and the others are opened or closed chromatically. For example, one would finger E, then open and close the keys of the foot joint to reach five tones between E and Eb.

In the complete microtonal scale, there is not a true homogeneity of sound because of the flute's construction. Certain keys will always close together. For example, the true F# key isn't depressed with a finger, but connected to a reachable key. Looking for a solution, the Dutch flute maker Eva Kingma built a full quartertone flute that is essentially a Boehm system flute with extra keys. The pluses of this are homogeneity of sound and a logical fingering system.

The discussion of microtonal resources, methods and practice has a strong new participant. Andrew Botros developed a website called *The Virtual Flute*.[32] Originally, this was a thesis project using data-mining to determine all of the fingering possibilities for altered timbres, fourth octave tones, trills, multi-phonics and microtones. The result was a massive 39,744 fingerings.[33]

31 The questionnaire respondents had not listed it as part of their studies and the author's wider personal experience has not shown any flutists who use it.
32 http://www.phys.unsw.edu.au/music/flute/virtual/main.html, Retrieved Feb. 14, 2013.
33 http://www.phys.unsw.edu.au/~abotros/thesis/, Retrieved Feb. 14, 2013.

The web service is an offshoot of Robert Dick's ideas, marking any given fingering's playability and timbre. The strength of this website is its practicality and exhaustiveness. There are many fingerings not found in *The Other Flute*. The first application allows the flutist to click on random keys and see all of the acoustical possibilities for that fingering. The second application allows a musician to enter any pitch or pitch-set and find all the possible fingerings for it. Botros has also taken variances with different flutes into account.

Microtonality is an extremely complex issue since it involves not only new fingerings, but also a new commitment to ear training. Tuning quartertones alone in the practice room is a necessary beginning, but only a beginning. There are computer-based programs that will play microtonal intervals in an effort to develop the ear but these lack the color and overtone components of live musicians. What is important to remember about tuning is that pitch is dependant on the source. Flutists probably have already intuited this. For example, many cannot, and do not, tune to the synthetic "A" sounded on a tuner. One notices quickly, that even if an oboist, pianist or anyone else matches the tuner's "A" exactly, when two musicians play together, tuning will be automatically adjusted according to color. The adjustment is very small, maybe one cent or two, but by doing so, intervals can sound more in tune than if one concentrates on matching pitch solely with the tuner.

As with many wind instruments, flutes cannot play microtonal intervals without a huge difference in color. This makes hearing and tuning the intervals much more difficult. Tuning and blending go hand in hand. To begin hearing quartertones, charting the tendencies of each tone can be of enormous help. That is, the flutist plays every tone in three possible dynamics and notates the tendency of the tone; too high, too low, difficult to play loudly etc. The short exercises of Pier Luigi Mencarelli and scales of Robert Dick are also helpful. One should note that knowing the tendencies of the flute does not provide the "answer" about pitch when working with other musicians. As stated before, pitch is dependent on the source. Adding in vast differences in color between different instruments makes tuning microtonal passages complicated. Developing this skill further requires that one have access to other musicians adept in this area.

Whether microtonality is an assimilation of ethnic musics or an extension of equal temperament in Western music, the sounds are fresh to our ears. All who are studying music should have an awareness of other tuning systems.

For musicians to move forward in step with developing compositional trends, listening along with practical lab or rehearsal experience is essential.

d. Rhythm

Similar to the discussion on notation, when a musician encounters new rhythms it would be wise to ask oneself why the composer has used such notation. It bears repeating that there is a difference between pieces that must be learned quickly for an upcoming performance and those that are transformative pieces bringing a musician to a new interpretive level. As background, several pieces could be considered prerequisites before studying more complex rhythms. *Le Merle Noir* by Olivier Messiaen is one. His use of *additive rhythm* insists that the flutist count the subdivision rather than the beat. Messiaen would irregularly add or delete note values, dots or ties to break from traditional time signatures. For example, there are two measures with 11 sixteenth notes, followed by one measure with seven sixteenths. The sixteenth notes must be exact as the flute plays in canon with the piano. In addition to that, the phrase should have an effortless floating character to it. Messiaen wrote with these rhythms to depict timelessness and they should not sound "counted." This is invaluable to internalizing a subdivision before taking on complex rhythmic ratios. Robert Starer's *Rhythmic Training*[34], a staple in musicianship classes, has exercises in polyrhythms that begin with two against three and three against four. As far as increasing complexity, the sky is the limit. For example, in Elliott Carter's *Double Concerto for Piano, Harpsichord and Two Chamber Orchestras* (1961) there are ratios as complex as 49:50. Translated, that is fifteen septuplets against twenty-one quintuplets at metronome speeds of 24.5 and 25.

The above example describes ratios between two parts. Polyrhythms in solo literature are counted as follows:

Figure 8: Rhythm Example 1

34 Starer (1969).

This means playing five 32nd notes in the time of seven with the whole unit equaling eight 32nds.

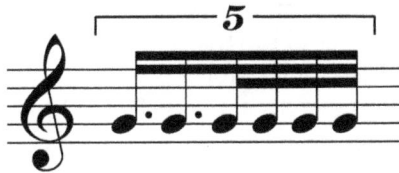

Figure 9: Rhythm Example 2

In this example one finds the equivalent of ten 32nd notes in a quintuplet.

Other challenges in new music are some of the newly invented time signatures used by Brian Ferneyhough. For example, *Superscriptio* (1981) uses 1/10 time.

Figure 10: Superscriptio, measure 1-6 © 1982 by Hinrichsen Edition, Peters Edition Ltd., London. Used by kind permission. All rights reserved

In order to figure out the speed of the measure, use the following calculation:

When the 8th note has a given value of 56 beats per minute, the 10th note equals 70. To arrive at that, do the following:

When $8 = 56$ and $10 = x$, cross multiply and the equation is $8x = 560$.

Then, $560 \div 8 = 70$.

To hear the length of the individual notes in a 1/10 measure; divide the speed of the measure by the number of notes in the measure.

Using the same formula, a 3/12 measure equals 84. If an 8th note $= 56$ and $12 = x$, then $8X = 672$. $672 \div 8 = 84$.

Looking again at the change from 1/8 time to 1/10 time, notice that reduced it is 1/4 changing to 1/5. Multiplying 4x5 we get 20. This means one can put 20 tones in a measure. Then divide the measure by 4 and 5 respectively to get the number of sub-beats in the 1/8 and 1/10 bar. 20 ÷ 4 =5; therefore, a 1/8 bar can be practiced with 5 sub-beats. 20 ÷ 5 =4; therefore, a 1/10 bar will have 4 sub beats. This 5:4 ratio can be practiced by playing quintuplets followed by the first four tones of the quintuplet. One could go through the entire piece with the sub-beats in order to internalize the speed of the measures before adding in the rhythms.

Concluding Remarks on Mental Preparation

Complexity begets growth and consciousness. The complexities of rhythm will force the musician to slow down and do the calculations. After that, the internal rhythm is strengthened. This task, while challenging, asks the musician to once again practice away from the instrument. There is pen and paper practice inherent in some of these challenges. Sight-reading is thwarted. The composer ensures that the performer is conscious during the preparation of the piece and is not merely imitating the "received wisdom" of teachers, recordings or colleagues. Even with the ease of access with recordings, I still feel that Ferneyhough has succeeded in making us conscious during the preparation of this work. This is not just music to be performed, but music to make us think. As said in the introduction, I feel that this energy, the energy in the performance of those who first tackled these scores, is the fire in new music.

In preserving the fire, this next section takes elements from this intense working process and gives them a structure. What new music was missing before was an expert model. Now we have plenty. The answer is not to insist that performers continue to apply brute force and dedication by taking the expert models away, but to identify elements in that intense process of self-discovery and structure them to lead to peak performance. The program I am applying comes from sports science, periodization.

Now that the mental preparation has been discussed, two different goals have been achieved. One, we've decoupled not only the musical score, but we've also decoupled our preparation process as well. We've become conscious of our interpretive autonomy. Two, what Ferneyhough called conscious and body-conscious, periodization calls low-wave and high-wave.

Mental preparation follows periodization's low-wave requirement. That is, practice at a low intensity regarding the demand on specific muscles.

This model gives a structure to the interpretive process that ensures both conscious and body conscious preparation.

V. Physical Preparation – Body Conscious Preparation

a. Stamina in Modern Music

Before we dive into the high-wave, or body conscious components of preparation, I am going to talk a bit about fitness and stamina. In 2010, I published a case study in *Medical Problems of Performing Artists*[35] that documented the higher physical demands found in new music versus traditional repertoire. The repertoire that inspired the study is from a group of composers using air as a compositional element, that is, all of the breaths are composed into the piece. Helmut Lachenmann, Nikolaus Huber and Heinz Holliger are some composers doing this. This is not unique to the flute as there are other works for other wind and brass instruments that use inhaling-while-playing and breath-holding as part of the music. The difficulty in this is that there is a build-up of CO_2 in the lungs when the breath is being held. This can cause a higher heart rate, an exertion headache and lowered cognition. Immediately after the extended breathing technique, the flutist might have an added difficulty in returning to the "normal" passages as the body seeks to recover from the stress. The heart will pound.

In the study, test areas from Heinz Holliger's *(t)tair(e)* were contrasted with test areas from traditional repertoire. To make the comparison more pronounced, the pieces from traditional repertoire were those notorious for breathing challenges, the *Scherzo* from a *Midsummer Night's Dream* of Mendelssohn and Debussy's *Afternoon of a Faun*. The difference between these examples and the Holliger is that the flutist still has a degree of control. Despite the long phrases and little time to breathe, the flutist can still control how resonant the phrase is and how much nuance is used. Ability might correspond to phrases that are more or less expressive, but it is not in the same category as Holliger where breathing is a composed and measured act in and of itself.

By focusing solely on breathing, I was able to gather enough data that showed that a higher VO2Max level was able to offset the challenges of the breathing difficulties and quicken recovery rates immediately following the breath holding. Traditional repertoire didn't benefit from increasing VO2max through exercise. Since stamina is measured by the amount of

35 Borkowski (2011) pp. 63-64.

VO2max a person has, we can conclude that the breathing techniques of breath-holding and inhaling-while-playing require more stamina than traditional playing does.

I want to take this chance to clarify what this study does *not* mean. I've seen several recommendations in print for flutists to get fit in order to improve their playing. Even in endurance sports, marathon running, triathlons and the like, VO2max alone is not a good predictor of superior performance.[36] There are too many other factors effecting outcomes. Looking at ourselves, we don't see things like military bands, whose musicians are more fit, playing significantly longer, more resonant phrases than symphony orchestras do. We don't see a correlation between a player's weight and their ability to phrase. We don't see smaller framed players running out of breath and bigger players having more resonance. We don't see phrasing deteriorating as we age. Our sound comes from our embouchures and resonance happens mostly in our mouths. The biggest case for this happened when Robert Dick brought circular breathing into play. He doesn't lose any resonance when he's playing with his "mouth only" air. Simply put, his embouchure is highly refined.

Flutists are sometimes misled when teachers advocate physical fitness to improve breathing. Perhaps this is impatience since rapid improvements in physical fitness are indeed possible. It might help, but if someone cannot perform the final passage from the *Scherzo* from a *Midsummer Night's Dream* in one breath, there are many factors to consider. Developing embouchure efficiency and tonguing efficiency without losing resonance is a process happening over years. Having a flutist take up running can easily leave her feeling disillusioned as to why the phrase still is not possible. There is also an obvious sensitivity with a teacher assuming which students are more or less fit. VO2max cannot be seen. It can also not be assumed according to a certain body type.

There are issues to consider when applying models from sports to music. My work focuses on flute fitness: embouchure strength and breathing exercises. I am not calling exercise bad. Exercise helps people live better lives. However, in sports science there is a distinction between health-related fitness and skill-related fitness. In my opinion, flutists prescribing running and aerobics

36 http://www.ncbi.nlm.nih.gov/pmc/articles/PMC3323922/, Retrieved April 1, 2013.

in order to improve breathing mistakenly assume that health benefits will improve skill. We are athletes of the small muscles, not the large ones. One must be very critical of any method and not merely assume that superimposing a model onto another practice scheme will yield the same success rates.

Back to new music and extended breathing techniques; does this mean that flutists playing these techniques need more stamina? In order to play the piece comfortably, yes. However, there are still a variety of ways to build stamina with breathing. Fitness is one of those ways. Flutists who are not able to work on their physical fitness have other equally viable options.

b. Periodization – A Model from Sports Science

When applying a method from any other field, it is important to apply it critically and not merely superimpose it on top of a musician's schedule. To further clarify the differences between health-related fitness and skill-related fitness, my specific application of periodization training is to develop the skill-related fitness needed to perform music with extended techniques. The goal of this is not to turn music into a sport-like activity, but rather offer practice plans that develop repertoire-specific stamina needed for a performance. With this heavy emphasis on sports, it is naturally concerning to me that some readers will take these recommendations and again confuse the difference between fitness for health and fitness for skill. My concern is that those who cannot exercise will feel at a disadvantage over those who can. I can put your fears to rest. While exercise is a known stress reducer and mood elevator, it is not the only way to reduce stress and improve mood. Running won't necessarily help you play longer phrases. Practicing supported breathing over long periods of time along while refining your embouchure will.

Periodization training is a program from sports science that systematically alternates work with rest so that the body peaks at the appropriate time. This chapter looks into the similarities as well as essential differences between music and sports. By following periodization, the performances, whether formal (a concert) or informal (a lesson), occur in a recovery phase. This ensures that a person has the maximum amount of energy available to deal with contextual interference, or the unexpected, in a performance. Periodized cycles can be created for a day, a week or when preparing for a monumental event, up to two years. This work originated by a Viennese endocrinologist named Hans Selye. Known as the father of stress research, Selye developed a model known as General Adaptation Syndrome.[37] General Adaptation Syndrome says that after an initial *stage of alarm*, a person will adapt to a new stress during the *stage of resistance*. When a specific stress doesn't alleviate itself, or when the body can no longer adapt, the third stage enters called the *stage of exhaustion*. Selye applied General Adaptation Syndrome to medical situations and in this instance the stage of exhaustion is essentially what causes death, that is, a lack of ability to adapt to life. In sports science, too much stress depletes energy reserves and the ability to perform will be less than it previously was. When performing in a stage of exhaustion, performance suffers. Periodization shows that when athletes train at a consistently high level of volume and intensity, there is a gradual decline in ability.

Periodization schedules, whether for days, weeks or years, follow similar wave patterns. They differentiate between practice volume and practice intensity. This is beneficial for two groups of people. Driven performers who always practice at the high volume/high intensity level never achieve their peak performance state because their bodies don't have an opportunity to perform at optimal energy levels. More relaxed players who practice at the low volume/ low intensity level are never pushing themselves to develop more stamina. The wave patterns work for both groups, and all of us in between. We push ourselves and we recover.

If I may chronicle my personal development for a moment and how periodization came into my own life, there are other lessons about music training to be learned. When I finished my undergraduate degree in music, I was a bit dumbfounded by how little I earned as a flute teacher versus what I earned teaching group ice-skating lessons. The ten years I spent teaching skating essentially paid for my professional quality instruments as well as travel to summer courses and auditions. I was a much more gifted flutist than skater and this didn't make sense at first. However, where a flutist could just hang up a poster offering lessons in a local school, the skaters required that teachers attend conferences on coaching and complete at least basic teaching certifications. Both musicians and skaters were essentially doing the same thing, teaching something they were very proficient in. The skaters

37 Selye (1952) p. 34.

were very organized and surprisingly, very well studied. I did my course-work at the Ice-Skating Science Development Center at the University of Delaware. The certification process led me to courses in sports science and after I was exposed to the physicality of new music, it seemed logical to apply the methods learned there. I do still wonder when music will catch up and develop a national center for the scientific study of music performance; invaluable work leading to higher performance levels while reducing over-use injuries.

Periodization Concepts

There are several components of periodization that are often missing from a musician's idea of practice. These new areas of exploration are

- Transition
- Tapering
- Overtraining

Transition

When using a schedule for a longer time such a few months or a year, the new work period begins with *transition* or *active rest*.[38] This means a time set aside for recovery from previous performances. Athletes might participate in recreational sports during this time. They might also take a vacation. Musicians, especially professional ones, often do not have this luxury. The year is not so neatly organized where one can plan a few weeks every spring for recovery. Nor are the most taxing points of any season so easily defined. When, however, a piece of extreme physical difficulty or complexity will be performed, most musicians could find a time to rest before beginning a new work as well as after the performance, even if "rest" means playing concerts with traditional repertoire. This plan could also be applied to a specific competition, a concerto performance or for a touring musician's appearance in a more important venue. In preparing for such a performance, a musician could use these concepts and schedule in rest or active rest to begin the preparation phase for a performance. This time is perfect for learning the notation and doing readings and listening talked about previously. This is also a time to learn any extended techniques without yet playing them in specific repertoire.

38 Provost-Craig (et al.) (1999).

This is also a time of practice away from the instrument that allows for muscles to rest. As seen in the previous sections, this work is not necessarily easy regarding concentration, but rather easy on specific muscles.

Taper

The second concept is *tapering*. Not only is this a concept that is often missing for musicians, but also the timing of it is worth noting. While writing this chapter, I talked to several musicians who said that they *do* taper off their work before a performance, adding that they practice very little the day before or the day of a performance. Athletes are tapering off their training weeks before their competition. Tapering off before a performance is a decrease in the volume of work, either gradual or sudden, while practicing at a high intensity level. For us, this means practicing with full performance energy. The periodization model suggests many at-tempo, full-energy sessions. During the tapering phase, there should be some time to recover free time allowing for creativity as well as enough days to recover sleep.

The main point of this phase is that one cannot practice at a maximum level all day, or the days and weeks before, and expect to be at a peak level for the performance. During this in-season time, the training that had been previously done will not be lost. You will actually feel a higher level of energy since you will recover some of what was lost. The tapering phase allows for increased creativity and the "letting go" that we all strive to achieve before a performance. To clarify, letting go means not only letting go of attachment to the outcome (results), but also letting go of a strict plan to allow room for ideas and inspiration. This paradigm shift in the tapering phase would transform the week or two preceding a performance from the common perception of this being a time of testing and anxiety into the most creative, energetic and inspirational time.

I am drawn to this concept for several reasons. First, musicians are often so hurried that the idea of taper seems like a luxury. Often, new scores are coming with short notice and we are performing them while we are still learning them. In contrast, if anyone has performed a work many times, you know the freedom that comes from this. Knowing a piece inside and out allows for creative play and spontaneity. In avoiding mediocrity and the "gig mentality" that Ferneyhough talks about, I am suggesting a reframe of our schedules. In solo situations this is certainly possible and even in ensembles, schedules could be adapted to allow for more run-throughs and a break between these run-throughs and the performance. I think we have it wrong. I've seen a sense of heroism when musicians have gotten through a performance with very little rehearsal. Again, addressing the very limited budgets we face, more rehearsal time is not necessarily needed. Time simply needs to be restructured.

Second, tapering off before a performance allows for more efficient muscle use. The neural representations of practiced patterns are recalled more efficiently. Research done on overtraining shows that when muscles tire, the brain will recruit less efficient muscle fibers to attempt the same task. This results in sloppy technique. Other theories from motor learning support the idea that too much frequency is detrimental to technique.[39] There is comfort in hard work and repetition; if I'm working as hard as I can, then surely I will perform well. We make an error, however, when we assume that adding up more and more blocks of error-free practice will mean better performances.[40]

Third, an added effect of tapering is a sharpening.[41] The mind is energized with performance-like situations where the musician consciously varies the length of the session. Performance flexibility and contextual interference are practiced before the actual event.

Another key in this is that simply reducing volume of training does not yield the same effect. The training volume needs to be greatly reduced while working at performance intensity. Performance intensity is something we repeat in practice rooms right before a performance over and over again. The change is to stop the "over and over again" in single practice sessions. There is an essential paradigm shift in letting yourself rest and recover prior to a performance that requires trusting your training and trusting the process. Look at what happens to runners.

39 Wulf and Mornell (2008) p. 7.
40 Ibid., p.19.
41 Noakes (2003) p. 307.

To taper effectively for a marathon runner takes about three weeks. Unfortunately, our self-confidence is fragile. Our egos require positive reinforcement of a hard workout every few days. If we take a few days easy- let alone three weeks- we go through withdrawal. Our distance runner's paranoia makes us fear that our muscles will turn to mush and that we will waste all those months of hard work.[42]

Tim Noakes recommends that "Once you decide to taper, do as little training as your mind will allow, but do that training at a fast pace."[43] Another essential difference between sports and music should be noted right here. A fast pace is not necessarily our goal. We are working towards the highest performance standard possible. Focusing too literally on the words of inspirational athletes could cause a student to play too hurried or nervously. Slow practice is also essential to our development. What Noakes is talking about is a mixture of achieving optimal performance and also settling into the realities of your performance abilities. Do it as best you can, but for as little time as you can. Play it once, at varied tempi, but play as if you are performing. The sharpening in this phase forces you to come up with coping strategies on the spot, exactly as you need to on stage.

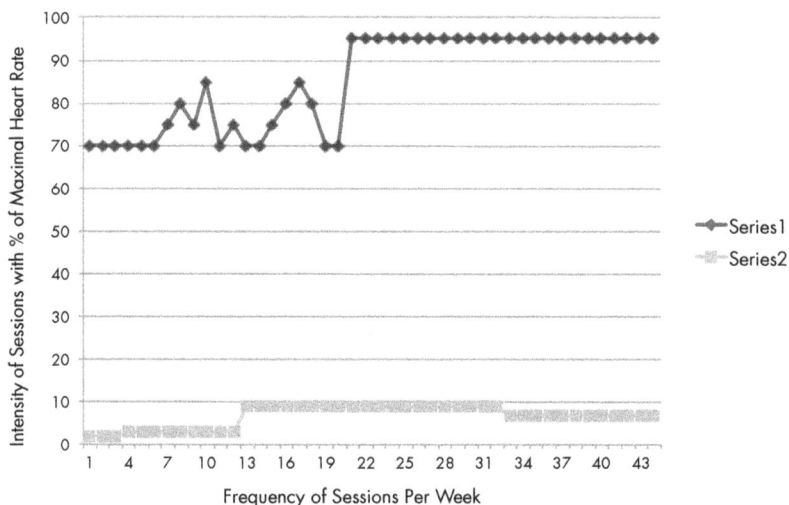

Figure 11: Periodization Yearly Chart (showing tapering off frequency of sessions per week)

42 Pfitzinger and Douglas (1999) p. 92.
43 Noakes, op. cit., (2003) p. 316.

There are not any specific recommendations for exactly how long a taper should be. Individuals need to figure this out for themselves. I believe that the discomfort with this is the outdated idea that we've been programmed to believe: more is better. We comfort ourselves with more repetition when there are volumes of research proving that this is not true. We've gotten it wrong. Ensembles rehearse at the last minute and pride themselves on having "gotten through." When we have advance time to prepare, we don't know how to structure that time and add in so much repetition that we are at risk for overuse and creativity is lost. We're exhausted, but exhausted for the wrong reasons. Hard work is good. When it is done well, it should energize us. When we are exhausted, we need to evaluate why.

Now, evaluating the volume of work and frequency of work is easy. Log hours in a day or sessions in a day. Evaluating work intensity is different. I don't believe it is so simple as to say slow practice is less intense than fast. In the forthcoming chapters, I will discus the physicality behind each extended technique, but this physicality is only true when they are handled in isolation. There are too many variables to create a teaching plan based solely on energy expenditure.

By keeping a log, I feel you can determine intensity. At the end of your practice, rate two things: your effort and your enjoyment. You should notice a difference when you are finished a high intensity practice session versus a low intensity one. When the enjoyment rating is low, it may mean that the work is too long, too intense or too monotonous. Training monotony is a proven risk factor for overtraining.

Overtraining

Moving from the log assessing both effort and enjoyment, we will now also learn to assess overtraining. Overtraining is fatigue that results in a loss of skill. There are two components of fatigue to think about.

Fatigue is an emotion. Sports science took a turn with the work of Tim Noakes, who called the traditional assessment of overtraining, the measuring of chemical changes and muscle inflammation, the "brainless model."[44] The new ideas coming out of fatigue research is that fatigue is primarily an emotion meant to protect the body from harm. At a certain point in exer-

44 Noakes (2008).

cise, fatigued muscles just stop. The difficulty is determining why. A bigger difficulty is having a teacher determine why. Noakes offers a difficult idea, namely, that cowardice exacerbates fatigue. There are obvious challenges when a teacher has to determine this and obvious mental battles to be fought in this regard. Noakes backs his idea up by analyzing the miracle of the end-spurt.[45] When an athlete feels the most fatigued, why is she able to give 10% more? The answer is that fatigue is not simply muscular or chemical. The will and the brain play bigger roles in deciding when exercise is finished. Simply feeling tired isn't necessarily a reason to stop.

Fatigue is also protective. This supports the idea that fatigue should not be ignored. It is serving a purpose. Athletes tend to exercise at a lower rate when they do not know how long a session will last. Open-ended exercise sessions show them holding some energy back. When they know how long and how far they will go, they are able to activate more muscle. This idea supports the planned practice sessions and planned intensity levels of periodization. In addition to this, an inherent sense of how much energy one has speaks to the need to listen to one's body as well.

Thankfully, when sports scientists rejected the brainless model of fatigue, they made concrete recommendations for assessing fatigue that are useful for us. Look for the following changes to determine when one is nearing the limits of stress tolerance.[46]

When a person is nearing his threshold of stress tolerance, you will see

- poor coordination
- more frequent technical mistakes
- a concentration span lower than normal
- desire to stop

When a person has exceeded his stress tolerance, look for

- mindlessness
- carelessness

45 Noakes (2012).
46 Interestingly, in some sports studies, the first ability an exhausted athlete loses is rhythm. They are talking about rhythm of a tennis stroke or a basketball dribble, but I believe this idea is worth noting. I can recall many instances where a student who was overwhelmed by a new technical passage and could no longer count simple rests leading up to the passage.

- an inability to concentrate on correcting mistakes
- an inability to understand mistakes
- abhorrence to training

In order to improve performance, nearing someone's stress tolerance level is not necessarily bad. As we've seen with General Adaptation, they will adapt. However, more frequent breaks are needed. If they do not get this rest, exhaustion will manifest in the above symptoms. This is the natural protective response to shut out further stimuli. Adaptation in this stage does not occur. Shutdown does.

When we reach this level, you can reduce any of the following to bring the intensity level back down

- reduce the volume of work
- reduce the complexity of work
- reduce the emotion in the situation

I'd like to make a quick recommendation for students reading this. When your teacher or conductor is not allowing you to reduce the volume or complexity in the work you are doing, especially when you feel put on the spot, do what you can to remove yourself emotionally from the task. Often, conductors are getting frustrated in these situations and emotion is skyrocketing. If you recognize that you have reached your threshold for stress tolerance, do what you can to center yourself. Briefly close your eyes and breathe to slow yourself down. Removing your own emotion will help. This is not an easy task to have such self-awareness. It might also help you to know that we have all been there. You might comfort yourself knowing that immediately after rehearsal there are many musicians to talk to who know how this feels. A quick acknowledgement of this might help you get perspective. Separate yourself from the task as best you can. In addition to this, the work of practicing control over your own energy will benefit you in difficult situations like these.

In contrast to athletes who measure practice intensity with heart rate monitors and stop watches, our practice intensity is somewhat subjective. It is also malleable. Our peaks are lessons, rehearsals and concerts. The rest of the time is (mostly) in our control. Through my years of reading about periodization for many different sports, I was not able to find any recommendations that look like a typical musician's rehearsal schedule, increasing intensity yet not reducing any rehearsal time before a performance.

Below are several periodization charts done on a weekly basis. The first thing to notice is that there is a lot of variance and flexibility in them. I do believe that this is different from varying practice by listening to your body. Many musicians do alter their practice by incorporating easy and difficult days, but this does not force you to push yourself on difficult days nor does it allow for the sharpening that happens when practice sessions are limited. Figure 12 is probably the most usual example of how musicians practice, a fairly intense week with Sundays off.

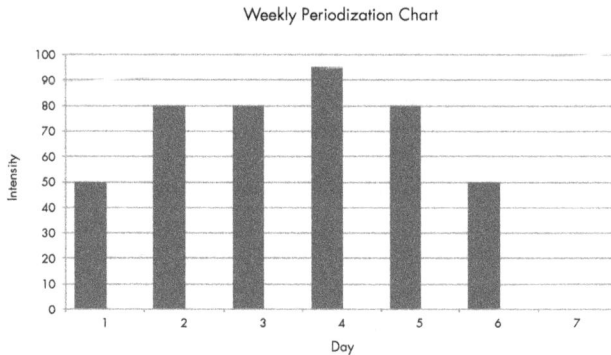

Weekly Periodization Chart

Figure 12: Periodization Weekly Chart 1 (after Bompa, T. O., 1999). *Periodization: Theory and Methodology of Training.* Champaign, IL: Human Kinetics, p.171

Figure 13 shows a weekly chart with two peaks, as does Figure 14. These would be interesting to experiment with, noting particularly the ease of performance felt on the second peak. Noting the differences in performance by comparing these two schedules might help a musician schedule practices before more important events. Figure 15 shows a few things. One, practice variability is evident. Two, the taper, even done during a single week, can be seen. There is a gradual build towards the first peak and a taper before the second. I can't help but think of how different this is from our usual rehearsal schedules. I think it would be an interesting experiment to change our open dress rehearsals, from the day before the performance to one of these other suggestions. Besides coming to the performance rested, the musicians would experience the sharpening during the easier rehearsals held right before the performance. When this is not possible due to scheduling, individual musicians might alter their other activities in order to follow one of these models.

Periodization Weekly Chart with Two Peaks

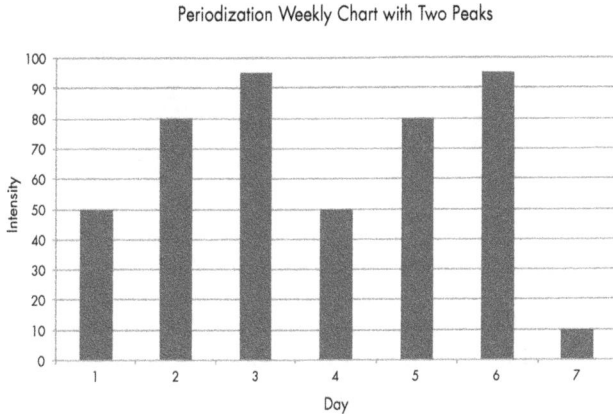

Figure 13: Periodization Weekly Chart 2 (Ibid., p. 172)

Periodization Weekly Chart with Two Peaks and Higher Demand

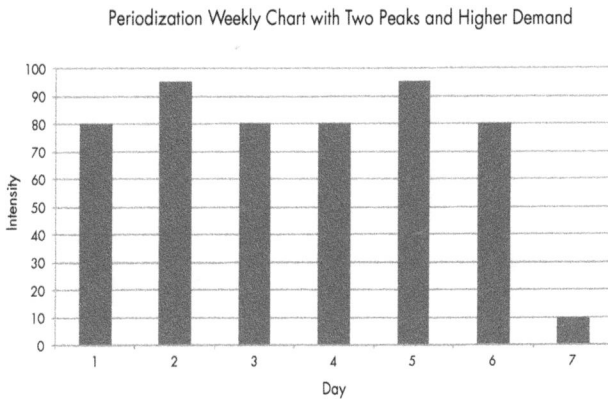

Figure 14: Periodization Weekly Chart 3 (Ibid., p. 172)

Two Peak Weekly Cycle Where the Second is a Competition

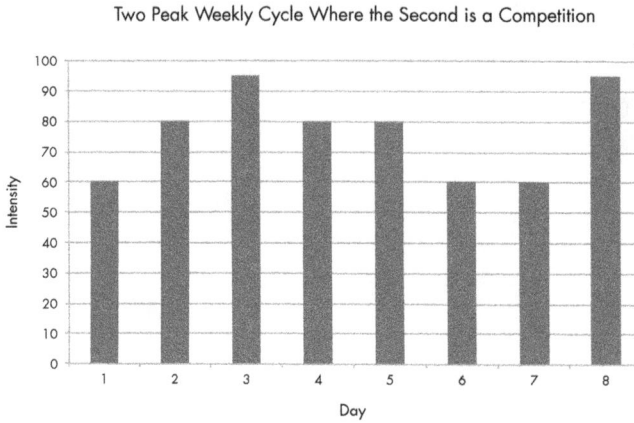

Figure 15: Periodization Weekly Chart 4 (Ibid., p. 173)

Look back through this chapter for a moment. It's about energy management. Having the ability, actually practicing the ability, to call upon the type of energy you need is an invaluable asset for peak performance.

Periodization is a complete idea that promotes peak performance while reducing risk of overtraining. The emphasis on practice variability and changing schedules opens space for creativity while preserving hard-won technique.

VI. Building Stamina Through Extended Techniques

The following sections place extended techniques on a continuum of difficulty. This approach assumes that the techniques are handled in isolation and is not meant to be exact, especially considering the myriad of possibilities in repertoire. This is a further development of the original idea I had when writing my dissertation. There is a well-circulated quote of Pierre Boulez about a student needing to jump with a miniature parachute into the contemporary world. At the time, I wrote the following phrase that inspired my work: "there are certain things that one may be willing to play, but cannot responsibly teach."[47] I felt the need for a systematic pedagogical approach and began with ordering repertoire in order to make the transition to new music earlier in a flutist's education as well as less of a systemic shock. When I first began in new music, online video tutorials weren't made yet. However, what happens naturally when things can be easily demonstrated is that we spend less time on them. I have heard a "you just go like this" type of approach. I wanted to make a progression for building stamina in order to show that there is a way in to this new sound world. In addition to this, I wanted to show that it does take time to develop the necessary skills to play these techniques artfully.

This progression also serves to further illustrate the concept of periodization. When planning high intensity and low intensity work periods, it is not so simple as slow and fast, loud and soft. With extended techniques, however, I think it is easier to place them along a continuum based on their physicality.

a. Embouchure Strength and Flexibility

Embouchure strength is ordered from easy and relaxing to extremely difficult with some fluidity in between. Most musicians who have taken the time to develop their embouchures through extended techniques notice greater dynamic variances, better control of pitch and an awakened idea of tone color.

1. Whistle Tones

"Whistle tones, or *whisper tones,* are lightly blown over the embouchure hole, resulting in lightly fluctuating tones in the very high register based on

47 Borkowski, (2008) p. 157.

the harmonic series."[48] In sound, they are similar to the sound of harmonics played on a violin, an extremely soft and whispery sound. On the flute in contrast, it is very difficult to hold a whistle tone constant. When playing in the third octave, the use of normal third octave fingerings helps to stabilize the tone. The overtones are no longer heard. While fingering the lower octaves, the harmonic series is heard like an improvisation because of the delicateness of the air stream. Performing whistle tones under stress requires still lips and quiet nerves. Breath support is not an issue here. The degree of control needed for whistle tones runs from extreme monk-like control to achieve exact pitches to a more relaxed improvisatory effect.

The rule for whistle tones is that the longest fingerings result in the greatest number of tones. That is, the low B (all keys depressed) results in 14 overtones. The C# (all keys open) results in only five overtones.

Anecdotally, Robert Dick described a competition between himself and Tom Nyfenger while he was studying with him at Yale University. By way of competition, Nyfenger challenged Dick to play the lowest whistle tone he could, and to Dick's surprise, Nyfenger was able to reach the lowest C on the flute. Unfortunately there isn't any recording documenting this. This supports the goal of Robert Dick's work, which was to document everything that is possible for the flute. Robert Dick continues to describe whistle tones played with vibrato, articulation and even a uvular flutter-tongue. These ideas first appear in *Tone Development through Extended Techniques* written in 1986.

Practical Application

Robert Dick teaches the control of whistle tone pitch in the same way he teaches control of harmonics. That is, the direction of the air stream dictates the pitch. The jaw moves, with completely relaxed lips, to determine the pitch. It is also helpful to use *throat tuning* and to practice by whistling or singing the desired pitch to find the appropriate throat position. The air stream must remain constant and in complete, relaxed control. Too much air simply makes an airy tone.

Practicing whistle tones is often advocated for warm-up exercises when one cannot find a practice room. Theoretically, the embouchure is in the ideal location for each pitch. In reality though, the lips are much more relaxed and the embouchure much more vertical than a normal playing position.

48 Levine, (2002) p. 15.

Concluding Remarks

Most students enjoy practicing whistle tones because of the ease of execution and the break they provide. They are probably the most relaxing technique known on the flute. I've put whistle tones on the lowest end of the periodization wave. When building embouchure stamina, whistle tones are the break in the work routine.

2. Glissando

Glissando is a borrowed technique from stringed instruments. While performing a glissando on a Boehm system flute is considered a modern technique, glissandi are also found on many types of other flutes. In *The Other Flute*, Robert Dick writes of the Boehm system, or modern, flute: "To my knowledge, the Boehm flute is alone in the plethora of flutes played worldwide in its traditional inability to make glissandi, and thus its adaptation to musical styles."[49] Nonetheless, new fingerings along with creative and good old-fashioned practice make glissandi an achievable goal.

Glissandi on the flute are divided into two categories, *embouchure glissandi* and *finger glissandi*. Both provide a chance for new tone colors and both provide new challenges in their execution.

Embouchure Glissando

Embouchure glissandi are played by changing the tension in the lips. The maximum interval that can be played by relaxing the lower lip is a quarter step lower. Another possibility is to turn the head joint either inward or outward, thus making the tones sound lower or higher respectively. Again, the interval that can be achieved is small, maximal a half step downward and a quarter step upward. Rotating the head joint also produces a change of tone color and resonance. Turning inward will darken the sound making the tone smaller and quieter, and turning outward will make the sound airy, though not necessarily louder. Glissandi can, therefore, not be substituted in works adapted from violin, for example. One can achieve the glissando effect, but the loss of resonance suggests that they are best played in a contemporary setting where composers can write them idiomatically.

49 Dick, (1989) p. 76.

The placement of glissandi on the periodization wave is very low. There is not an issue with embouchure strength but embouchure flexibility. The more flexible the embouchure, the greater interval that can be achieved. This is especially true when rolling the headjoint outward. Other embouchure work, specifically harmonics, develop flexibility that can be applied to embouchure glissandi.

Finger Glissando

The possibilities of finger glissandi depend on the type of flute. The closed-holed flute is at a great disadvantage. The flutist must gently depress the keys with a highly refined sense of touch. There will be a sudden change of pitch and tone color when the key is finally closed all the way. The difficulty of playing this way is that there isn't a buffer zone as there is on an open-holed flute. Faster glissandi are much more challenging because of the delicate pressure on the keys.

I must quickly comment on how my thoughts have evolved since I began this project. In my dissertation on this same topic, I had written a few paragraphs discerning a true glissando from a glissando effect. A glissando effect was where the limits of the flute meant that two tones could not be reached without a bump in the middle, for example, between C2 and Eb2. I suggested altering the pitch as far as possible and covering the change of fingers with vibrato or other nuance. I wrote this before I had time to play with The Virtual Flute website. This changed everything! With over 39,000 fingerings to choose from, I am indeed able to connect those two tones. There is a color change, but in the context of the piece, *Tenderness of Cranes* by Shirish Korde, it worked quite well. The piece is full of imagery of birds in flight and evokes an airy Japanese shakuhachi sound. The altered fingerings added to this color and made complete glissando possible. Previously, I used a harmonic fingering, from C1 to Eb1. The ring keys can be vented while staying on a low C fingering, making a complete glissando. The change in sound from an overblown C1 to a vented fingering sounding Eb2 is immense. The harmonic sound of the C is more dense and focused than normal, and the vented fingering for the Eb is more airy than normal. Now, I finger low B with the first finger on the left hand open to make an airier C that matches the Eb in tone color. One could experiment with this, to find the most musical solution. In fact, this is the work of studying a contemporary score. One must decide what colors and imagery work in a given situation, finding a well thought-out solution, balancing the technical work with the interpretation of the piece as a whole.

As just mentioned, playing glissandi only with traditional fingerings is limiting. Nonetheless, there are lessons to be learned about touch by doing so. I've been in conversations with composers with many misconceptions about the possibilities of glissandi on flutes. The above example fit into the pictorial nature of the piece but there are others where the color change of alternate fingerings would disrupt the musical idea. Therefore, I am going to discuss finger glissandi for the situations when they are needed.

Robert Dick and jazz flutist Steve Kujala have mastered a closed-hole glissando technique by using a new sense of touch. Another reference to this possibility is the "Victorian glide" or "rush."[50] Flutists in the Victorian era were playing closed-hole flutes and were able to glide upwards over two-octaves. What should be noted in the two examples here is that jazz flutists can control how and when they play a glissando. A Victorian glide was played on a closed hole flute, but with only eight keys. Flutists facing new scores can best approach this by developing a technique for a glissando effect and using the Virtual Flute for alternate fingerings.

Open holed flutes, while easier for some glissandi, still have drawbacks. One slides the fingers on or off the holes in the keys first then lifts the outer ring of the key.

With traditional fingerings, glissandi are possible in four tone groups:

C#1 to B2, C#2 to B3, A2 to F#3 and D3 to A#3. From these four groups, shorter glissandi can be used.

Glissandi on the piccolo, alto flute and bass flute are a bit more complicated. They don't have ring keys that can be slowly vented. One must learn a new technique combining an embouchure glissando, a tone color change, vibrato and a new touch on the keys and altered fingerings.

Concluding Remarks

Despite the complications with playing many glissandi, there are valuable lessons to be learned. The first is, playing glissandi forces flutists to think

50 http://www.larrykrantz.com/faqflute.htm, Retrieved March 3, 2008.

about re-developing their sense of touch. Second, it is chance to experiment. This is chance for flutists to think critically about the limitations of the technique and apply it in the most musical way.

3. Vocalizing While Playing

Singing and Playing

Singing and *playing* is a technique that is exactly as it sounds. One vocalizes while blowing air across the embouchure hole. The difficulty is not in the execution itself but in its complexity. Normally, a vocal line will be notated beneath the flute line and the two will be played simultaneously. This technique is probably the most telling about a flutist's inner hearing skills. As flutists play single line melodies, hearing polyphonic lines is often an underdeveloped skill. Finding the correct pitches is the first challenge.

Becoming more physically aware of the vocal chords while playing is a good step in learning more about projection. Related to singing and playing is *throat tuning*. By singing internally, the vocal chords are set for the corresponding pitches. This strengthens inner hearing, and according to some, produces tones with an optimal resonance. One can test throat tuning by randomly singing the pitches aloud to see if they match the pitch being played.

Speaking and Playing

The discussion of the use of the voice cannot go further without also introducing the practice of speaking and playing. A flutist will speak either directly into the flute tube or across the embouchure hole. Both methods will produce words that are somewhat distorted.

The most essential and accessible work for developing these skills is *Voice* (1971) by Tōru Takemitsu. Besides some spoken text, Takemitsu gives absolute vocal freedom. For example, "with voice, humming shouting, singing, etc."[51] There are not any other indications except for dynamic markings. One has free choice of pitch, vowel and/or consonant and the color of the voice. Other instructions are to speak into the instrument with the lips almost entirely covering the mouthpiece and to speak normally. Although this is a

51 Takemitsu (1971).

classical composition, one should be aware that Takemitsu also wrote many film scores including the score to the film *Ran* (1985). Beginning here can give the student an idea of the theater and mood of his work.

Moving into the score of *Voice*, marking all of the vocal tones with colored pencil would help outline the architecture. The difference between having a performance simply full of original noises and one that is well designed is the difference in understanding the form of the piece. Then, the vocals can be consciously chosen within a larger framework. The pretext for Takemitsu's *Voice* is that during the piece, the flutist encounters a ghost. The interpretation follows from here. One can decided to do this with any range of emotions; fear, anger, sadness, humor.

A good step to learning this piece is to think of the possibilities of the voice in general. One could begin by listening to pieces that explore the extremes of the voice. More accessible to students might be the work of Erin Gee. Her *Mouthpiece* cycle (2000) has a somewhat pop feel while she uses her own voice in an innovative way. Gee was a student of Beat Furrer who explores the use of the voice to produce new instrumental timbres. Relevant to this interplay of voice and instrument is his *auf tönernen füssen* which was recorded by Carin Levine. Although this piece post-dates *Voice*, it can be used in the studio to open the ears to vocal possibilities. Further work experimenting with vocal sounds can be done via the International Phonetic Alphabet. This system categorizes all the sounds in the known languages.[52]

Although the following pieces do not give the freedom as Takemitsu's *Voice* does, they can certainly be used in exploring the resonance of the flute with various vocal sounds. Beat Furrer and Bernhard Lang have both used extensive vocals integrated into their compositions.

Furrer's *auf tönernen füssen* (2001) is a piece for amplified flute and spoken voice. During the piece, the two parts should fuse together to make one sound. Furrer uses the vowel sounds to not only change color but also pitch.

---

52 Erin Gee has written a dissertation using the international phonetic alphabet to describe extended vocal techniques. *The Relationship of Non-Semantic Vocal Music to the International Phonetic Alphabet and Research in the Phonetic Sciences: Brian Ferneyhough, Georges Aperghis and Dieter Schnebel* is available in the library of the Universität für Musik und darstellende Kunst Graz.

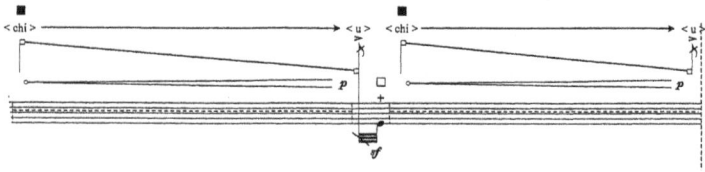

Figure 16: Beat Furrer, *auf tönernen füssen*, page 3, line 1 © 2001 by Bärenreiter-Verlag, Basel. Used by kind permission

The flute offers a supporting role to the poem, coloring some of the words as follows:

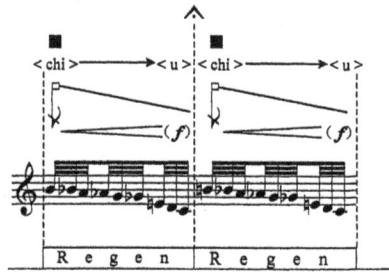

Figure 17: Beat Furrer, *auf tönernen füssen*, page 4, line 3 © 2001 by Bärenreiter-Verlag, Basel. Used by kind permission

Bernhard Lang in *Schrift I* (2003) for solo flute writes the desired syllables exactly in the score. For example, one speaks a "te, ke, ti, to" which alters the color of the *pizzicato*.

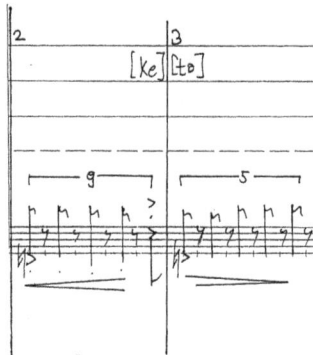

Figure 18: Bernhard Lang, *Schrift I*, measures 2-3 Reprinted with the kind permission of Zeitvertrieb Wien Berlin

Concluding Remarks

Where some might find this work fun; experience shows that most flutists find it difficult. Flutists work on developing beautiful, bel canto sounds and immerse themselves in learning established traditions. When one is learning a performance practice, the individual "voice" is often stifled. It is no wonder that some might feel lost with such freedom. In the studio, the first obstacle to overcome is shyness. These techniques offer flutists the widest creative freedom since their beginning of the instrument. This can be threatening. Where teachers previously have guided the students into what type of sound they are looking for, now it would be wise to let all that go and give them a chance to explore their own voice. Begin this work by reminding them of what such a challenge can accomplish. To paraphrase Peter Röbke, the central pedagogical question of new music is, "what does this music bring out in me that other music does not?"[53]

4. Multiphonics

Multiphonics are directly derived from string techniques. They are related to double stops on a stringed instrument. They use altered fingerings plus an altered embouchure position. The roots of multiphonics for flute extend well before the end of the Second World War. In the 19th century, the Dutch flutist Georg Bayr experimented with mutilphonics. (His book *Doublenotes for Flute* was published in Vienna without a date.[54]) His ideas are the forerunner for many of the common multiphonics used today. In the 20th century, the Italian virtuoso Serverino Gazzelloni experimented further. Other published materials include Pier Luigi Mencarrelli's *New Sounds for Woodwind* (1969), Thomas Howell's *The Avant Garde Flute* (1974) and Robert Dick's *The Other Flute* (1989). The total work left over 1000 multiphonic fingerings with intervals ranging from a minor second to an octave and a fifth. Andrew Botros has augemented this further. Although the Virtual Flute outdoes the other methods with its practicality and ease of use, it is nonetheless important to understand the capabilities of multiphonics before this website can be fully used.

---

53 Röbke, op.cit., (2000) p. 117.
54 Dick, op. cit., (1989) p. 83.

The following three rules apply to multiphonics production:

1. The larger intervals are reached more easily
2. Most multiphonics can only be played softly
3. Articulation reduces the response of the multiphonic[55]

Both Robert Dick and Carin Levine have created large tables which detail the qualities of the intervals. They are complete with recommendations for composers regarding the difficulty or ease of the interval, and in which dynamic they are possible.

Every fingering on the flute yields at least one multiphonic. Multiphonics are based on three types of fingerings: *harmonic, chromatic* and *microtonal* fingerings.

Multiphonics based on harmonic fingerings range from the flutes lowest B to middle D. The intervals possible include the perfect fifth, perfect fourth, major third, minor third, and major second.

The intonation in these is not very accurate with fifths being too large and fourths too small. Correcting intonation with multiphonics is extremely difficult as one can only use the lips, and the lips are already stretched beyond a normal playing position to reach the interval. A delicate change in the air stream could help intonation with normal fingerings but would disrupt the production of both tones of a multiphonic.

Multiphonics based on microtonal fingerings (those venting half holes in the keys) result in a parallel microtonal scale. When using the Virtual Flute, it is possible to select any two tones on the flute and get a number of possible fingerings. When experimenting with possibilities, however, it is helpful to note that multiphonics are possible with microtones and harmonic and chromatic fingerings.

Multiphonics are dependent on the type of flute one plays. A "B" foot joint, a split "E" key, or open or closed keys will alter the fingering one must use.

Practical Application

When one over blows, one can reach an octave by lengthening the embouchure to accommodate both tones. To reach a multiphonic, the jaw and

55 Ibid., p. 84.

lower lip define the lower pitch, and the upper lip finds the upper pitch. It is wrong to attempt to use two different air streams. Only one is needed with an aperture large enough to produce both tones. In reality, beginners do this all the time. While trying to find the middle octave, they often play a ghost of the first octave at the same time. Even for advanced flutists, this is the easiest way to start.

For other intervals, I've found it easier to reach both tones by using a beginner's biting or smiling embouchure. For more difficult intervals, one can oscillate between the two tones until the stability is found to hold them both together. When one is beginning multiphonics, oscillating between the two pitches is done almost like a change of tone color. The upper lip moves in slow motion and one is forced to concentrate keeping the lower lip and jaw stationary. This requires extreme embouchure precision for some of the more finicky intervals. Through this process, the lips become more flexible for changes in tone color in the standard literature. Another method is setting the air stream for a non-played middle tone. For example, for two F's an octave apart, the embouchure can be set for a C or D in between. One also becomes keenly conscious of the space inside the mouth, the vowel one speaks, and the tuning of the throat.

A further use of throat tuning is applicable here. This is when one sings a tone to set the vocal chords to the desired pitch. In traditional music, one often does this often unconsciously in order to strengthen the resonance. With multiphonics, one can use this technique by singing the weaker pitch of the multiphonic so that it speaks more easily. One would then remove the singing, leaving the throat set for the desired pitch.

When I was thinking about placing multiphonics on a periodization chart, I was torn. This technique is so varied that it is difficult to say if this requires more embouchure strength. Many of the intervals are touchy and require not so much more strength, but rather embouchure precision that is not noticeable in many other techniques. Multiphonics also develop embouchure flexibility and variability. There are many multiphonic intervals where embouchure stillness must be so exact in order for both tones to sound that this is indeed very tiring. My feeling is that in attempting to hold lips so still that they do tend to become more tense.

5. Altered Fingerings and Harmonics

Altered Fingerings

The use of alternative fingerings for normal pitches is gaining acceptance. Sometimes called "fake fingerings," this detracts from the development of the flute's sonic capabilities. Orchestral flutists and more often, piccolo players will use a harmonic fingering to flatten the pitch of an unusually sharp note. For the alto and bass flutes, the third octave is almost always played with a harmonic fingering. The normal fingerings are much too sharp. Alternative fingerings also offer many more possibilities for dynamic contrasts. It is normal, for instance, for an orchestral flutist to use both fingers 1 on 3 on the right hand for a high F to facilitate tuning. Many flutists use alternative fingerings on the piccolo regularly, adding the trill key for a soft high E, for example. Studying alternative fingerings gives orchestral flutists many more possibilities for tonal exploration as different overtones are highlighted.

In using alternative fingerings, a widened palette of tone color results. While harmonic fingerings are often pale and flat, alternative fingerings, according to Robert Dick, come in five categories:

- Normal-pitches have very strong fundamentals, strong second partials, and progressively weaker third and fourth, fifth, sixth, seventh and eighth partials.

- Diffuse-pitches have strong fundamentals, strong second partials, fairly weak third and fourth partials, and extremely weak fifth, sixth and seventh partials if they are at all present.

- Muted-pitches have fairly strong fundamentals and weak second and third partials. If any higher partials are present, they are extremely weak.

- Bright-pitches have strong fundamentals, very strong second partials, strong third partials, and progressively weaker fourth, fifth, and sixth partials. Higher partials may be present but are extremely weak.

- Edgy-pitches have fairly strong fundamentals and extremely strong high partials.[56]

56 Dick, (1989) p. vii.

The Virtual Flute webpage uses similar groupings for a tones color and play-ability. As mentioned earlier, there are almost 40,000 fingerings and the site is easy to use, interactive and educational. Botros takes variances of flute models into consideration. Practicing these new timbres opens the ear for creative color changes in traditional repertoire. One will hear degrees of piano that were not possible with normal fingerings. The embouchure will have already adjusted with the new fingering, which makes the dynamic range bigger just by having played them. Both guides lend themselves to play, experimentation and an enhanced sense of tonal color by handling altered fingerings in isolation. Both these guides make altered fingerings a topic of instruction separate from repertoire.

Harmonics

Harmonics, sometimes called *flageolets* or *overtones*, are more familiar when played by string players. A violinist will use flageolets regularly in classical repertoire. For a flutist, he or she fingers a fundamental tone and over blows until a note from the overtone spectrum sounds. In the normal flute fingering system, overtones are the basis for the upper octaves. For the second octave one over blows an octave without changing fingerings. For the third octave, one over blows an octave and a fifth with modified finger-ings to facilitate tuning. In new music, the use of the overtone series and harmonics has grown considerably, asking flutists to over blow two octaves or more, sometimes with a first octave fingering.

It had been an experiment of Robert Dick's to find how high the flute could go into the fourth octave. He found that an acoustical limit was G in the fourth octave, and most flutists find the fourth octave with normal finger-ing extremely taxing on the lips. He recommends only short practice of the fourth octave to avoid fatiguing the muscles. I agree wholeheartedly. I use these to illustrate the extreme of practice intensity, placing them at the high end the continuum. These should only be done on high intensity days. In Sal-vatore Sciarrino's series of pieces *L'opera per flauto*, one finds harmonics in the fourth octave. In this example, one sees that composers can easily push flute techniques further than what flutists would normally think of themselves. Reaching pitches in the fourth octave is difficult; but, adding a first octave fingering makes them one of the most physically demanding elements in flute literature. The length of the phrases and difficulty of the pitches makes this work virtuosic beyond what had been previously imagined.

Such an extreme breath support is needed that some flutists count on an adrenalin rush to achieve the pitches. The diaphragm is under such stress, pushing as hard as possible over and over again, that the several flutists who performed the piece said it made them nauseated. In actuality, the piece was probably performed before enough time had passed to develop proper embouchure strength for these intervals. Going back to a theme mentioned in the introduction, I feel that the pioneers of new music, those who learned without the help of teachers and tutorials, had a deepened commitment to the works being performed. I feel that the time taken to understand a score and understand the imagination of a composer shows in a performance. To exemplify this, I encourage you to look up recordings of the *Hermes* movement of *L'opera per flauto*. Roberto Fabricciani played the original recording and accurately plays the multi-phonic harmonics. There are many other recordings on YouTube where you don't need to look any further than the first chord. Many players approximate the pitches and have settled for an effect. This serves to remind us that new techniques take dedication. When we don't give them time to develop, the same way we give our embouchure time to develop, the music takes on a mediocrity and loses its fire.

Practical Application

Harmonics exercises teach one how to hold the lips, how much air pressure is needed, and how much one needs to correct intonation. These exercises are meant for orchestral flutists to develop a better sense of pitch, tonal control and flexibility. They are, however, a perfect springboard for the harmonics that one finds in new music. One must experiment with the room inside the mouth to control the pitch. Most harmonic fingerings are very flat and orchestral flutists would correct pitch while allowing the harmonic to sound with an airy tone quality. This gives the lip muscles time to develop. Another reason for this is that the true fingering is the one that will be performed. The practice of the harmonic is merely a stretch of the lips beyond what they would be called to do in an orchestra. Many composers of new music, however, write harmonics when they want a paler tone.

Robert Dick also recommends harmonics practice for the development of the tone and embouchure. Pitches with an optimal resonance have only one embouchure position, and that is the same position of the mouth while playing a harmonic. The position is a combination of the lips, jaw, throat and space

...side of the mouth. When one practices the harmonics, one should avoid turning the head joint inwards, but should rather push the jaw forward. This teaches the correct breath support for the tone. Otherwise, one achieves a pale color, most likely piano, but without resonance and proper intonation.

One example of Robert Dick's harmonic practice is the *Partita in a minor* BWV 1013 by J.S. Bach. One always uses the lowest fingering possible, and when the wrong tone sounds, it shows that the embouchure wasn't in the correct position. Harmonics are problem solving in this way. The mistake becomes very obvious. Teachers use tricks to have students hear this mistake. With traditional fingerings one can play a G2, and then move to E2 without moving the embouchure at all. The E will sound, but without the best resonance possible. Teachers will depress the additional keys so that E will sound without the student knowing when. The student can more clearly hear the lost resonance when the lips are unprepared for the new note. When one uses harmonic fingerings without moving the embouchure, a completely wrong note in the overtone series will sound. This trains the ear and mouth to place each tone more precisely.

Figure 19: Robert Dick, *Tone Development Through Extended Techniques*, page 22. Reprinted with the kind permission of Robert Dick

One can also practice scales with harmonic fingerings on every tone possible. The difference in intonation is heard immediately in this context. Other ideas for development of control are practicing harmonics with single and double tonguing, and at various dynamic levels for variations of tone color and resonance.

Concluding Remarks

Practicing harmonics helps strengthen the embouchure and refine the ear. They also open up the ear to other color possibilities. This technique comfortably bridges the classical and contemporary worlds. These are also techniques used in extreme. Extreme dynamics with harmonics require time to build embouchure muscle. This is another technique, like flutter tongue, that can no longer be considered "new." It is integral to developing a resonant sound and the benefits for embouchure strength and flexibility are noteworthy. The sooner the embouchure has a chance to develop the strength and flexibility for harmonics, the more accessible the repertoire will become.

6. Fourth Octave

Playing above high C should also become a standard practice for serious flutists. Daily studies should eventually incorporate these upper tones. Getting there requires some embouchure development. Some fingerings are easier than others. For example, I find the D4 easier than the C#4 while E4 is extremely resistant.

Before these tones can be played musically, play them in short bursts and don't try to sustain them. The embouchure will tire quickly. Until the strength is there, think of this as weight lifting, lifting a maximum weight a few times then taking a break until another practice session.

When we've gotten used to high C being the highest tone, the fourth octave can seem out of reach. Try to remember how much time you took to develop your third octave and give it at least that same amount of time. A difficulty for some flutists at this stage is that they are used to playing with a good sound. The fourth octave takes that feeling away for a while. However, when returning back down to high C it will be that much easier to control.

I've placed the fourth octave and fourth octave harmonics on the high intensity end of the continuum of the periodization schedule. These techniques need short bursts of practice with rest in between. Eventually, when they become second nature, they can be integrated into daily practice.

7. Trumpet Embouchure

Trumpet embouchure is quite a scandal in the flute world. Some hate it, saying it should never be written or played, others seem fine with it. To play this, one buzzes the lips into the tone hole of the head joint or directly into the flute tube with the head joint removed. Achieving different pitches comes from varying lip tension and shape of the mouth.

. the lips is intense because of the small size of the tone hole. ...ler than a trumpet or even a french horn mouthpiece. Anyone ... d it will say that it disturbs the embouchure. The lips tingle or itch ... n feel slightly swollen. This makes it difficult to play a clear tone immediately following. The key in practicing trumpet embouchure is to do it for very short periods of time. Also, following the weekly periodization model, I would suggest only practicing trumpet embouchure on high intensity days to allow for both muscle building and muscle recovery.

Putting trumpet embouchure on a continuum, beginning with buzzing the flute body without the headjoint is easiest. Because this is so difficult, do not buzz into the mouthpiece until buzzing into the flute body can be done for at least a short musical phrase and without feeling a loss of embouchure sensitivity afterwards. Then, one can move to buzzing into the embouchure hole. Start with short bursts of sound on high intensity days and work until the desired phrase can be played *and* music can be made afterwards.

Even more intense than blowing a trumpet embouchure through the mouthpiece is to do this while inhaling. This is difficult even without a flute, but it is possible to get the flute to buzz at pitch while doing this. Heinz Holliger's *Lied* is the most virtuosic example I have seen of this.

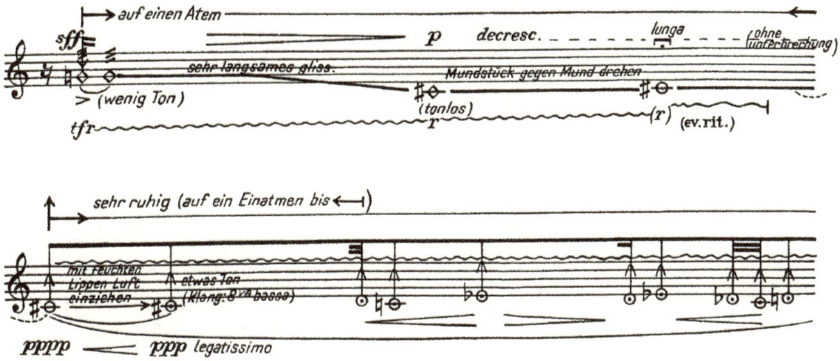

Figure 20: Heinz Holliger, Lied, lines 3-4 Heinz Holliger LIED © 1983 by Schott Music GmbH & Co. KG, Mainz, Germany. All Rights Reserved. Used by permission of European American Music Distributors Company, sole U.S. and Canadian agent for Schott Music GmbH & Co. KG, Mainz, Germany

b. Extending Articulation

1. Flutter Tongue

The oldest extended technique, now considered a classical technique, is *flutter tongue*. All flutists pursuing a professional career in any degree program will encounter this. It is required of every flutist with a symphony orchestra position, as it appears in orchestral literature early as Richard Strauss' *Don Quixote* (1896-97).

The two types of flutter tongue are the *rolled tongue* and the *glottal* or *uvular* flutter. They differ in speed and pressure, resulting in different dynamics and expression. The rolled tongue is generally faster with more pressure, moving the air faster through the flute. This makes it more suitable for the high register. The *glottal* or *uvular* execution is therefore better for the lower register and quieter tones. It is possible to use both types, even in one phrase, switching from one to the other without a break.

Robert Dick's criticism of the use of flutter tongue among flutists is that it isn't used creatively. It is either turned on or off like a faucet, much like a beginners first experiments with vibrato. One usually hears it played loudly, with the tongue moving very quickly. The tone is usually distorted with a lot of excess air and the pitch is usually sharp. Carin Levine agrees with this point, reiterating that it is possible for flutter tongue to be played *espressivo* in every dynamic and register of the flute. The markings of flutter tongue, however, do not ever specify any variation of speed, but one can easily find flutter tongue written in extreme dynamics and in the opposing registers of the flute.

Robert Dick's experimentation with glottal flutter tongue has lead to fascinating results. He is able to achieve a flutter with minimal pressure so that *multiphonics* or *whistle tones* can also be fluttered. In addition to this, Dick is able to articulate with the tip of the tongue while fluttering. To date, I have not yet come across a piece requiring this skill.

Robert Dick has said that he always uses the glottal execution. He finds that it works throughout the entire range of the flute as well as in every dynamic level. Most flutists find the glottal execution in the upper register very difficult. The tendency of playing in the upper register with the required increase of support, air pressure and tightened embouchure seems counterintuitive to an open flutter in the chest. Many flutists close the throat trying to get air to move quickly enough. This makes the uvular flutter move up too high in the throat, and thus too fast. The result is only a distorted tone not a true flutter effect. This may be only psychological, but a challenge nonetheless.

Practical Application

Uvular Flutter Tongue

To develop a uvular flutter tongue, Robert Dick recommends gurgling practice. By gurgling with water, one can feel the glottis active. One then works with less and less water, until the mouth in empty. Gurgling without water is essentially what the glottal flutter tongue is. It is also possible to trick the mind, gurgling without water, by holding the head back as if water were there. Then one can bring the flute to the lips with the head still back, until the muscles learn this movement in an upright position.

Some flutists trouble shoot by accumulating saliva in the mouth and gurgling it into the flute. This has many drawbacks, the main one being excess saliva afterwards. There is often not sufficient time to gather it and sustaining it through longer phrases is impossible. Also, this creates a tendency for the larynx to come too high. When this happens, the flutter is too fast and what sounds through the flute is simply an unclear tone. Solving this problem, one can use the method of Carin Levine. Begin with a breath of air, as deep as possible in the chest and with the throat as open as possible. By placing a hand on the chest, the resonance of the air can be felt. The flutter should then remain under the larynx, and although it feels extremely slow, it sounds very fast. When this method is not working, it is helpful to begin the flutter by inhaling. This can then be easily transferred to exhaling and then blowing into the flute. One should practice this flutter on a very comfortable note on the flute such as low G. The process of inhaling with an open chest produces a more relaxed flutter tongue in contrast to the previous approach. Gurgling with water doesn't prevent the flutter from coming up too high and can even encourage it. Practicing with the head back is an interesting psychological tool to help transition the flutter into the flute but flutists may have to work again at keeping the throat and chest open.

Robert Dick's gurgling practice has yielded a flutter tongue that can decrease in speed. Using more or less pressure and more or less speed, he achieves a flutter with varying expressive qualities. A decelerating flutter mixed with a decrescendo, is another creative use of flutter tongue.

I have developed a consistent uvular flutter tongue by practicing the sounds while speaking. When I speak some words with a French "r" I can practice having my mouth in the correct position. Because I am not a native French speaker, the sounds do not come naturally for me and sometimes the rolled "r" does not sound. If I transferred this to the flute, there would be a delay before the flutter would start. The vowel I use preceding the "r" is decisive for me in getting the French "r" to sound.

Fluttering With the Tip of the Tongue

To practice the rolled "r" the student should place the tip of the tongue on the soft palette of the mouth and relax the sides so that some air comes through. There is a tendency to put too much pressure on the tip of the tongue, resulting in very short flutter that cannot be sustained.

I also developed my rolled "r" by speaking. Before I was able to do so, I could've been convinced that this was genetic. It is not. Practice works. Personally, I began with short bursts of flutter and then gradually extended them. I also noticed a common problem when trying to roll my r's in speech. When using an American "r" I can feel a reflex to put my tongue back in my mouth touching my back teeth. If I find myself in that position, the flutter won't work. I need to lower the back of the tongue first. From there, I noticed different vowels make different amplitudes and pressures of the flutter. For example, the Spanish word *tierra*, using an "e" sound, uses a flat tongue and has a lower, gentler amplitude. A word with a "u" sound can be played with a higher amplitude and lot more pressure. This was my beginning in developing a flutter that is variable and expressive.

While working with students, one should be flexible in the approach. Some students can flutter tongue well in the upper register, some only on the low. Some have a very easy time rolling the tongue while others cannot do it at all. This comes from the difference in language exposure and different strengths with flute playing all together. Exercises can be built based on tone studies so that the flutter tongue can be expanded through the range of flute. Some students can flutter very well, but cannot sustain the flutter though a long passage. Apart from an urgent performance, there is no need to rush the development of flutter tongue. Therefore, work with their strengths. A student who can flutter short tones can begin as such:

Figure 21: Jennifer Borkowski, *Flutter Tongue Exercise 1*

and then work on extending the flutter throughout the range of the flute.

Those who can flutter longer can use regular tone exercises, beginning from a point of comfort and working either upwards, downwards, or outwards.

Figure 22: Jennifer Borkowski, *Flutter Tongue Exercise 2*

Beyond that, it would benefit all students to work on a flutter moving in and out of a tone. This is an often challenging task because of its explosive nature. Flutists often find that they need much more air to sustain the rolled tongue. Practicing this way helps develop a lighter roll. The rolled "r" in the throat will not work without the appropriate mouth position. If anything is too closed – mouth, throat or chest – it won't sound. Moving in and out of straight tones can pinpoint and help fix this problem.

Figure 23: Jennifer Borkowski, *Flutter Tongue Exercise 3*

Concluding Remarks

These exercises provide the opportunity to work on flutter tongue while allowing the muscles to naturally develop. This saves students from facing it for the first time in a piece, or worse, in a piece that they are already scheduled to perform. Often, one will notice impatience with modern techniques. Some students will give up much more easily than they would with regular tone or scale studies. The point here is that these techniques take time and can be taught. Whether or not a student dives into the world of contemporary techniques, all will encounter flutter tongue. All would benefit from short but daily exposure.

2. Tongue Ram

A *tongue ram* is a percussive effect that gets its name from ramming the tongue into the embouchure hole. The dictionary states that to ram is to "cram or stuff."[57] If I had to further qualify this technique, beyond an extension of articulation, I would call it a diaphragm technique.

Because the embouchure hole is covered, a tongue ram will make the flute sound a major 7th lower. An alto flute and bass flute will sound a minor 7th lower and the piccolo a minor 9th lower. These facts are to keep in mind when transposing works between the different flutes. Both pitches are most

57 Ram, http://dictionary.reference.com/browse/ram, February 25, 2008.

often notated, the top one being the fingered pitch, the bottom the sounding pitch.

Practical Application

The word "ram" is often used when describing car crashes as in "she just rammed right into me!"[58] That about describes the energy it takes to play a tongue ram. The flutist should blow with a "hoot" sound, ending with the tongue either inside the embouchure hole or inside the mouth behind the teeth. This feels like playing the flute backwards as flutists usually use a "tooh" to articulate. The resonance comes from very forceful diaphragm movements. One can experiment by varying the end position of the tongue, ending through the lips or by staying in the mouth. The trick when pushing the tongue into the embouchure hole is to keep it somewhat covered with the bottom lip. Keep the flute in a normal playing position then roll it inwards. If the bottom lip is below the back edge of the tone hole, the tongue ram won't sound. Another possibility is to start from a normal playing position, roll in, and then *inhale* the tongue back into the mouth ending on the roof of the mouth. The key here in getting this to sound is energy. The tongue ram needs a fast and forceful motion. A score will not specify how it is to be played. Factors regarding speed and dynamic should inform this choice. Tongue ram is often played without a microphone, and this should also inform the player as to how much diaphragm motion is needed to get an acceptable volume level.

A common mistake is trying to re-tongue after the tongue ram is finished. This backlash can be remedied by practicing the tongue ram in a mirror without the flute. One can watch that the tongue stays between the lips when it is finished. Simply forcefully stick the tongue out and stay there watching it in the mirror.

Repeated tongue rams will immediately show how difficult this is. Try to play a simple melody with tongue ram to feel how much work this is for the diaphragm.

3. Pizzicato

Pizzicato is a percussive effect for the flute that leaves much room for interpretation. There isn't a rule as to how pizzicati should be played. Carin

58 Ibid.

Levine's book divides them into tongue pizzicati and lip pizzicati, as do many composers. To play pizzicato, one holds the flute in playing position and uses a much more explosive attack that stops short of a normal stream of air across the embouchure hole. The volume is much less than a normally blown note. After one has mastered the execution of pizzicato, there is a lot of room for experimentation. Often, composers won't notate whether a pizzicato should be done with the lips or with the tongue.

Practical Application for Tongue Pizzicato

A tongue pizzicato is played by holding the tongue tightly against the roof of the mouth, holding a pocket of air behind it. When it is forcefully released, a percussive sound is heard resonating across the embouchure hole. There are as many variances with the sound as there are variances in the shape of the mouth. Since the air doesn't run through the length of the flute tube, the shape of the mouth has a huge impact in the quality of the sound. An open sound such as an "ahhh or an "ohhh" will create much more resonance. The mouth itself will resonate sound since the air has not moved very far from it.

In addition to this, one can also vary the consonant articulated by the tongue. Any consonant involving the tongue is possible. T and K are the most natural as they are used in normal articulations. The can be softened to D or G sound, or one can experiment with a Ch or J sounds as well.

Pizzicati with more resonance use a softer consonant. For less resonance and a sharper attack, use a harder consonant.

When the tongue is tight against the roof of the mouth, the effect will be shorter and more percussive. However, it doesn't expel much air forward. Using a looser tongue can move some air forward but without the "pop" that comes from the intense pressure of the former example. One must decide what each individual piece of music needs.

Composers Beat Furrer and Bernhard Lang write pizzicati with vowel sounds. Experiment with this without the flute. By changing the vowel sound in your mouth, you can also change the pitch. One could use ka, ke, ki, ko, or ku, for the end position of the mouth. The vowel would not be spoken, or even blown, but the flute would resonate differently. Composer's experimentation in this regard informs the rest of the work. When there isn't an indication of what vowel to use, you are free to chose. This makes playing this technique that much more expressive.

Practical Application for Lip Pizzicato

Another pizzicato is done with the lips. Again, this is often not specified in a score. To do this, the flutist holds air inside the mouth then explodes the lips with a strong "pa" sound. The same principle applies as for tongue pizzicati. Looser lips give more resonance; tighter lips make a crisp attack.

Another factor influencing the choice of pizzicato is the speed of the passage. A lip pizzicato is very slow and cannot be repeated very quickly. Tongue pizzicati are faster but need more preparation than normal tonguing does. Normally the tongue bounces off of an existent air stream. Here, one needs to regroup between each one so that the right amount of pressure on the roof of the mouth can be created. Pizzicati with double tonguing are certainly possible but the resonance would be greatly diminished.

Tongue ram and *pizzicato* also teach a valuable lesson about resonance. Achieving resonance without air running though the length of the flute is a challenge for many flutists. This work offers the chance to build strength and use more energy. Diaphragm-push and articulation strength are enhanced by practicing these techniques. The ideas learned about resonating with the mouth will continue to enhance understanding about their ability to project.

c. New Uses of Air

1. Air Sounds

Air sounds are simple. Air sounds played musically are not. The work of Toshio Hosokawa informed my teachings on air sounds. He uses exact symbols to show the ratio of air to tone.[59]

Practice this making a difference between a focused sound without any air escaping and move gradually to a full air sound without any tone. Practice will teach you to differentiate between 50/50 air to tone ratio and 70/30 or 30/70. Getting air sounds to project and playing different dynamic levels takes some experimentation.

---

59 See Figure 7.

Another air sound is an audible gasp. Heinz Holliger writes plenty of these. They are certainly not difficult by themselves. The difficulty lies in the fact that they *are* indeed the breath for the following phrase. We will get much more into that when we look at Holliger in depth in the forthcoming chapters.

2. Jet Whistle

A jet whistle is a strong air attack that mimics the starting of a jet engine. The embouchure hole is completely covered and the flutist forces air through the tube with a strong air stream and diaphragm impulse. The same principal applies for jet whistles as for whistle tones, the longer the tube, the richer in overtones the sound will be. That means, when a richer tone with more resonance is needed, a lower fingering should be used. Often, fingerings are not notated.

Jet whistle also uses vocal sounds, or vowel sounds to alter pitch or tone color. From a historical viewpoint, composers have been long experimenting with the voice as a new development of tone color.

Practical Application

While playing a jet whistle, one can alter the pitch by altering the vowel sound formed by the mouth. Moving from an "ooo" to an "eee" sound, the tone will ascend an octave. Moving from an "eee" to an "ooo," the tone can descend an entire octave. In addition to that, one can raise the pitch by turning the head joint outwards. The flutist plays the jet whistle with the entire mouthpiece inside the mouth, completely covered. Moving it back behind the teeth, there is still room to rotate the head joint so that the keys remain flat, not rolled inwards. Doing so will raise the pitch and increase the amount of overtones. Likewise, rolling the keys inward will lower the pitch. One can also alter the pitch by using an ascending scale pattern. This lessens the overtone component, which may not be enough noise for a jet whistle.

One cannot sustain them over much more time because of the massive quantity of air that they require. A flutist will expel all of the available air in one quick impulse. Therefore, jet whistle wins the honor of being the first extended technique presenting flutists with serious issues of stamina.

Repeated jet whistles need all of the acoustic tricks mentioned above. One simply does not have time to expel all of one's air, over and over again. One can experiment with rolling the head joint at a given speed to create more noise. The use of vowel sounds is certainly possible. The issue is again, stamina. The diaphragm must move much more strongly then in traditional playing, and much more quickly.

I was ready to crown Salvatore Sciarrino "king of the unplayable jet whistle" until I met him. He writes jet whistles over 32nd notes played over several lines of music. His idea of the sound, though, is different from the loud, shrill scream of most jet whistles. He sees them as more body sounds, less flute sounds. This difference makes them entirely playable. He has an almost John Cage-like acceptance of extraneous noise, calling it organic. The repeated jet whistles found is much of his music can be practiced without the flute, changing the shape of the mouth, *almost* whistling, until one can create a musical effect. Then, putting this back into the flute isn't the impossible task that it looks like.

Whatever the setting, jet whistles will wake you up. They need much more energy than any traditional technique that I can think of. Placing this along the intensity continuum, I have to put this technique on the samle level as the fourth octave and trumpet embouchure, although jet whistles do not require recovery time for muscles to rebuild.

3. Circular Breathing

The comprehensive book on circular breathing is *Circular Breathing for the Flutist* by Robert Dick (1987). Without simply reiterating what he has said, the intention of this chapter is to strongly recommend his method. He systematically describes each phase of circular breathing. Circular breathing involves squeezing air out of the mouth with the cheek muscles while simultaneously inhaling through the nose. The biggest challenge is maintaining a clear tone with the "mouth only" air. This involves strengthening the cheek muscles and refining the sides of the embouchure to sustain the tone. When one circular breathes well, it is not possible to tell when it occurred. During the few seconds when the flutist inhales, the air is coming only from the mouth. The connection to the chest and lungs is cut off, causing one to rethink the ideas about a flute tone needing an open throat and chest. This is not meant to encourage closing the throat and chest, but rather to highlight how much resonance is possible when one uses the shape of the inside of the mouth to its maximum.

Circular breathing enables the flutist to play extended phrases which can be used in modern or traditional repertoire. An added benefit of learning circular breathing is an increased ability to play convincing diminuendi and pianissimo passages because of the strengthened cheek muscles.

Robert Dick asserts that with daily practice, circular breathing can be learned in two months.

4. Inhaling While Playing

A fairly common trend in new music is inhaling through the flute. This is another technique requiring a much higher stamina level. In order to get enough resonance, one must inhale a great volume of air and often very quickly. The difficulty lies with the fact that there is a loss of control over the phrase. When a composer writes in the inhalation, it is generally not allowed to take a normal and relaxed breath to get back on track. Another problem is having too much air through repeated inhalations. This leads to a build-up of carbon dioxide in the lungs which causes a rise in heart rate. Inhalations can be combined with vocal effects, articulations and buzzing lips.

Concluding Remarks About New Uses of Air

New uses of air in modern music often take away a flutist's control. The body is pushed physically. Mental and perhaps psychological challenges about sound and resonance force the musician to think about and use the body in a new way. The benefit for the rest of a player's flute playing is invaluable. The more ideas about resonance one has, the more expressive one can be. When breathing is no longer limited, the more creative the phrasing can be.

riodization of Heinz Holliger's (t)air(e)

Once the required techniques for a more difficult piece have been built, we are going to look at periodization applied over a longer time period. Periodization was helpful on a weekly basis. We differentiated between high and low intensity tasks to build stamina, muscle and flexibility. One situation that musicians repeatedly have trouble with is structuring larger time frames. We're generally misguided, adding up more blocks of repetition for security. Any flutist who has stepped into the orchestral excerpt track has probably experienced this. The challenge is not to play the excerpts, but to keep them fresh.

Periodization does not erase repetition altogether, but differentiates between repetition that is helpful and repetition that is not. The goal of periodization at this time is to prepare thoroughly yet recover enough lost energy to peak in time for the performance. By adding practice variability, we reduce the probability of boredom. We also reduce the possibility of panic because of a loss of skill. Loss of a previously established skill signifies overtraining, not too little training.

The following sections take apart this piece to set up a work plan for a performance.

a. Breathing Challenges

This is not the first piece of Holliger's to focus on air. Air, in this piece, is composed. You don't get to chose when and how to breathe. He chose it for you. This piece is one of several from a time when a group of German composers were breaking the barrier between the performer and the public by way of physiological experiment. They were making us human. *Atem*, means breath in German. Consider the following titles from this time, *Atembogen* and *Pneuma* of Holliger, *Atem* of Mauricio Kagel, *Atemzüge* of Dieter Schnebel, *Air* and *temA* of Helmut Lachenmann and *Res-As-Ex-Inspirer* of Vinko Globokar. They ushered in a paradigm shift of compositional elements. By composing with air, they are composing not only for an instrument, but for an energy. Holliger's writing insists on body-consciousness. There isn't any other way around it. He asks you to sit in discomfort, breathing only when you absolutely have to. Pay attention to your breathlessness and increase it. This is a paradigm shift for us in a huge way. We spend our conscious energy on calming ourselves down during a performance. The rush of adrenalin and physical discomfort is something we usually try to avoid, or at least ignore. I've written in another book on this topic, using Holliger for stress inoculation.[60] After all, if you can pay attention to your discomfort during a performance and still get through this piece, everything else will seem easy.

The breathing challenges are in their organization. He writes a series of alternating inhalations and exhalations with breath holding in between. He asks you to empty the lungs and then hold the breath as long as possible, inhaling only when it becomes absolutely necessary. Then hold the breath while filled with air, exhaling only when necessary. This causes a build up of carbon dioxide in the lungs. Carbon dioxide in the lungs causes an increased heart rate and stresses the vascular system. This causes pressure in the head and ears. Think of being underwater and the quickened breathing that is done when you surface. The subsequent phrases can feel very difficult because you are still recovering. The more that this is trained, the faster the recovery will be. Other instructions are "with the last of your air"[61] and "do not breathe"[62]. Inhalations are notated by an upwards arrow on the note stem. He has written inhalations through rhythms and articulations, through audible gasps and through repeated and rhythmic audible gasps. He asks you to wait for seven seconds without breathing. Finally, he allows, "breathe in unnoticeably."[63]

60 Borkowski, *op cit.* (2012).
61 Holliger, (1988) p. 1.
62 Ibid. p. 1.
63 Ibid. p. 1.

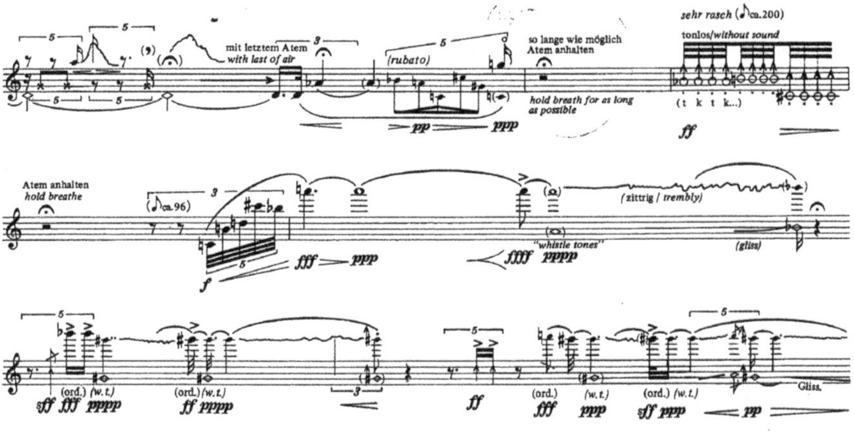

Figure 24: Heinz Holliger, *(t)air(e)*, page 1, lines 4-9. © 1983 by Schott Music GmbH & Co. KG, Mainz, Germany. All Rights Reserved. Used by permission of European American Music Distributors Company, sole U.S. and Canadian agent for Schott Music GmbH & Co. KG, Mainz, Germany

This does not give the flutist complete control over how much air to take in. The first real breath isn't until page four, line twelve with the fermata standing alone. That is the first chance for the flutist to take a relaxed and controlled breath. The rest of the piece continues without other breathing challenges until a short reprise of ideas towards the end.

When the teacher plans the work period for this piece, the breathing work should come early on. What can be learned from an athlete's multi-lateral, or cross-training approach is that practice can start without the instrument. Using a metronome and visually scanning through the piece, the flutist can practice all of the breaths alone. A technique that is very valuable is to "play" the piece through a normal drinking straw. The flutist can articulate through the straw and listen to the air by itself. This shows how much air is being used. The benefit of this is to focus solely on breathing so that muscles develop and the body is conditioned with minimal stress. Isolating the breathing in this way allows the flutist to work harder on breathing than he or she normally would since other factors aren't in the way. The sections could be divided until the smaller sections feel under control. At that point, the flutist would combine them together.

During this phase of practice, fingerings, rhythms and other techniques should be practiced without the breathing requirements. The flutist should breathe whenever necessary. As was seen in the periodization models, hard work was always balanced out. When isolating the breathing work, the flutist will feel tired. In time the body will adjust. On the longer periodization charts, this work falls into the off-season; learning new elements. To increase confidence with the breathing sections, the player could practice sections back to back, without a pause in between. This is helpful but one needs to remember that this is done in advance, at the latest, in what would be the pre-season phase. At this time, the player should also have developed enough control over technical passages.

1. Breathing Work by Multi-lateral Training

Another possibility is to cross train and build overall endurance. As was seen in my study mentioned in section Va., increasing VO2max did help the breathing challenges in this piece. This was done by increasing aerobic capacity. What happens in this piece is similar to anaerobic conditioning. The word anaerobic means "without air, or without oxygen."[64] Anaerobic exercises are short and intense, not lasting longer than a few minutes. Athletes use these to train for when they do not have enough oxygen. For example, a runner will add short sprints into a jog in order to build endurance. The exercises would begin for short intervals of time, between thirty seconds and one minute, with about the same time of rest in between. This would be increased to two minutes with thirty seconds rest. Short explosive exercises like jumping rope or sprinting accomplish this. The high-intensity phase should be long and strenuous enough that a person is out of breath and recovery periods should not last long enough for their pulse to return to its resting rate.

A word of caution, the point is not to jump around and then try to play the piece. That only adds stress. One puts the body through a similar stress so that it adapts. Simulate the situation, but certainly not with the flute in hand. While this is a direct route to conditioning oneself for the fastest recovery time possible, it cannot be recommended for all flutists. It is also not the only way to meet the breathing challenges.

64 Anaerobic exercise: Energy without oxygen, University of Iowa Healthcare, http://www.uihealthcare.com/topics/exercisefitness/exer3098.html, Retrieved February 25, 2008.

One could also work with a breath builder. These small, portable machines work with a resistance knob on the end so that one breathes in and out through the mouthpiece with an increase in resistance. Breath builders[65] have been used by patients recovering from various lung illnesses as well as by elite athletes. They increase lung capacity. By increasing lung capacity, endurance is greater. When one has been exercising, one could certainly add to the intensity of the routine. When a breath builder is already being used, one could increase resistance. Starting from scratch with such methods over a time period that is too short *could* add unnecessary stress. These examples are therefore meant as an example of what is possible regarding multi-lateral training.

b. Building Embouchure Muscles

The next area of work in *(t)air(e)* is building new embouchure muscles. One needs complete embouchure control until the very end of the piece. The *pppp* found at the end with harmonic fingerings is an example. One cannot risk fatiguing the muscles earlier in the performance. With a trumpet embouchure occurring well before this, we see the necessity for building abilities slowly.

This trumpet embouchure, or vibrating lips, is done while inhaling. In the explanation of symbols, the upwards arrow means inhale. Using principals of overload,[66] the flutist can begin with short bursts of sound and gradually increase the number of times this is done in a practice session. At first, five attempts would fatigue the lip muscles. Immediately after, relaxed first octave passages should be practiced. Once the sound is achieved, the flutist can practice lengthening it until the required four seconds is reached. The difficulty with this limited amount of allowable practice is that there is limited time to refine the embouchure and experiment with the most economical way to produce the sound. This can be thought of in advance of an attempt so that a) the muscles relax in between attempts, and b) there aren't any wasted attempts. As with all high intensity exercises, this should not be done every day.

---

65 http://www.powerlung.com/region/us/powerlung/compare/, Retrieved April 17, 2013.
66 "Overload" traditionally means doing more today than you did yesterday. When one can do this, "training" has occurred.

c. Fingerings and Other Techniques

To learn the traditional aspects of the piece, one would read through as if none of the extended techniques are there.

Another area of developing lip control is the the standard whistling moving into whistle tone on page four, lines six and seven.

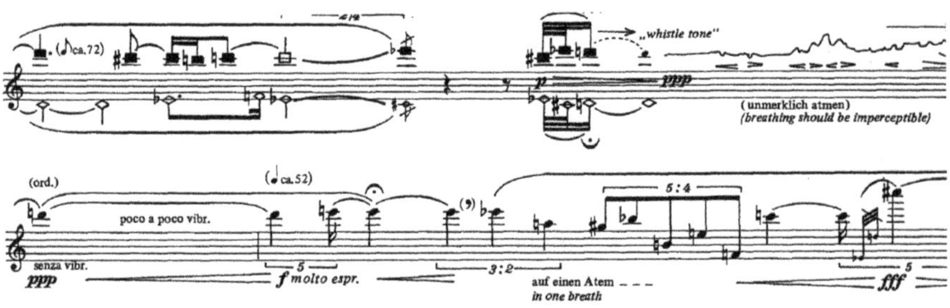

Figure 25: Heinz Holliger, (t)air(e), page 4, lines 6-7. © 1983 by Schott Music GmbH & Co. KG, Mainz, Germany. All Rights Reserved. Used by permission of European American Music Distributors Company, sole U.S. and Canadian agent for Schott Music GmbH & Co. KG, Mainz, Germany

This is a fingered D whistle tone moving into a sounded D. The transition should be seamless. A lot of embouchure work coupled with singing and playing make this possible. This is a wonderful piece to strengthen the embouchure overall. The whistle tone passages are not fatiguing like the fourth octave and trumpet embouchure are. The lips are more relaxed than usual and this can be practiced in any given session without worry of a training schedule.

The table allows for more than enough time for the fingerings to be learned while breath support and stamina are being developed.

Table 2: Jennifer Borkowski, *Periodization Model for Heinz Holliger's (t)air(e)*

	Stamina Work	Embouchure Work	Finger Technique
Preliminary Period or Active Rest *Two to Three Weeks Duration*	Divide up the work areas. Preparatory listening and reading work. Cross referencing other works of Holliger.	Beginning extended techniques practice, experimenting in addition to practice without the flute.	Slow controlled practice of fingerings without extended techniques.
Early Preparatory Period *Four to Six Weeks Duration*	Stamina building, breath holding passages. Daily practice without the flute, increasing work while decreasing rest.	Begin with whistle tones and alternate days with work on trumpet embouchure and fourth octave practice.	During regular practice, tempi are increased and extended techniques are gradually added.
Late Preparatory Period *Two Weeks Duration*	Put sections together, back to back run-throughs of small sections to continue building stamina. Increase to run-throughs of larger sections with less rest in between.	Begin to taper embouchure work, fewer repetitions. Whistle tones continue without change.	Refine finger technique.
Preconcert Period *Two Weeks Duration*	Trial run-throughs of the entire piece for teachers or colleagues. Back to back run-throughs of the entire piece should be avoided now.	Continue to taper embouchure work.	Technique is secure allowing the emotions to become honest.
Performance *One Week Duration*	Performance.	Embouchure work is finished.	Technique is prepared and emotions are honest.

Concluding Remarks

All of the recommendations above are guidelines and this does not mean that any one individual must follow them exactly. What has been described is the theory, and this theory can be put into practice in a number of ways. Foremost, the time frame can be lengthened up to as long as six months. One must follow the proportions and adjust their personal calendar. Also, if someone does not find trumpet embouchure fatiguing, there is not a reason to practice it in a limited way. Some flutists will come to this piece with plenty of experience in the fourth octave and not find it difficult. Others need to begin from the ground up. The guidelines are there so that the majority of flutists can be reassured that their muscle fatigue is normal. They also have a plan for working through the problem. What multi-lateral training does is set the work area away from the music. When one only works with the instrument, the repertoire itself becomes a test. Periodization eliminates this aspect of practice. It does not mean that the performance will be perfect or even easy. The periodization theory seeks to eliminate overuse injury, mindless repetition and unproductive stress. The theory shows the performer how to come to a performance ready and rested while the training period builds positive stress experiences. Considering the extremes of still whistle-tone control, inhaling trumpet embouchure and breath holding in this piece, the "nuances of energy expenditure"[67] Ferneyhough mentions, come to life.

67 Ferneyhough, op. cit., (1998) p. 369.

VIII. A Periodized Daily Studies Program

Many flutists who specialize in modern music have commented that they do not use extended techniques in daily studies. They probably get enough of a work-out since they are playing repertoire using them very often. This is not true of most flute students or professionals who do not play much new music. Learning the techniques only when they need to be performed causes unnecessary stress on the body and mind. Assimilation in daily studies is a must.

I have assigned the following techniques a value based on the physical energy level they require. The values are as follows:

Flutter tongue: 4	Polyrhythm: 2	Air sounds: 5
Harmonics: 5	Pizzicato: 7	Whistle tones: 1
Jet whistle: 10	Tongue ram: 6	

These levels are based on a scale of 1 to 10, with traditional playing lying between 3 and 5. Eventually, some of the levels will even out as the techniques become better trained. Flutter tongue and harmonics will become second nature as the muscles learn to play more efficiently. Constants in this list are jet whistle, tongue ram, pizzicato and whistle tones. Jet whistle, being an "anti-flute" technique, is meant to free up the performer not only with fresh breathing, but also from other confining thoughts. An option is to add in an improvisation after the jet whistle. The player can chose how much energy to spend during the improvisation.

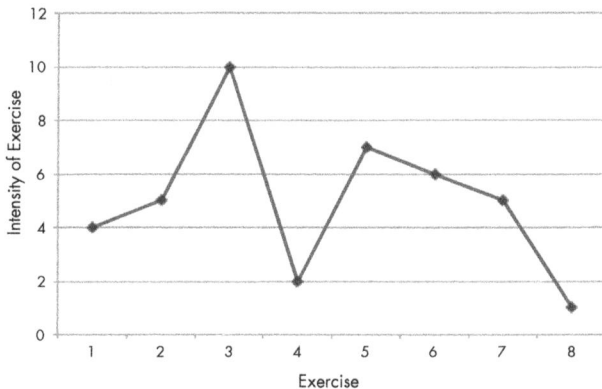

Figure 26: Jennifer Borkowski, *Periodization Micro-Cycle Line Graph*

Periodization charts of work and recovery follow this type of pattern. Short term charts are geared toward maximizing rest and recovery, while the long term chart (Table 2) is geared toward "peaking" for an optimal performance. Both systems, however, follow a wave-like pattern. The latter simply finishes the wave in a downward turn so that the body is recovering lost energy for the peak phase.

The practice plan assimilates the levels above and also follows wave-like patterns. These exercises end purposely on a down-turn since this is only one component of a flutist's daily work. The flutist can decide how to structure the rest of the practice session based on periodization concepts.

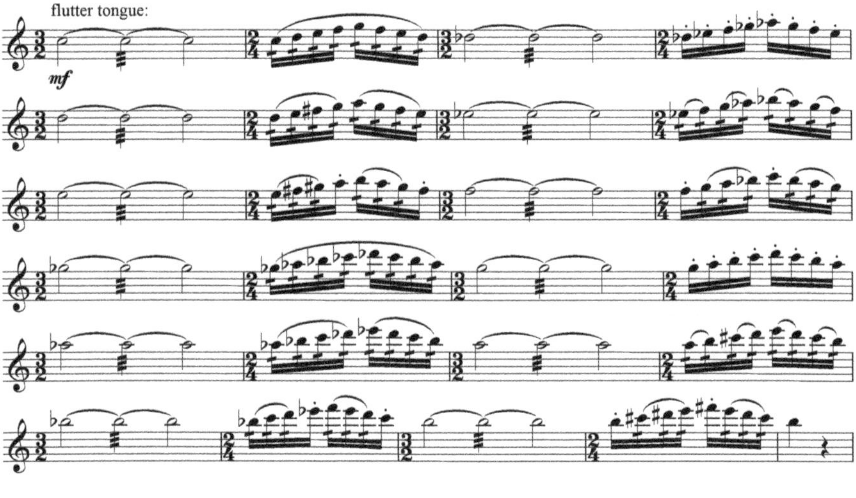

Figure 27a: Jennifer Borkowski, *Periodized Daily Studies Example*

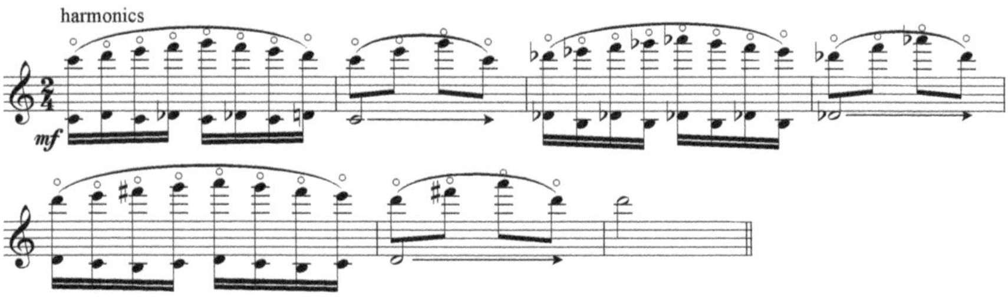

Figure 27b: Jennifer Borkowski, *Periodized Daily Studies Example*

Figure 27c: Jennifer Borkowski, *Periodized Daily Studies Example*

Figure 27d: Jennifer Borkowski, *Periodized Daily Studies Example*

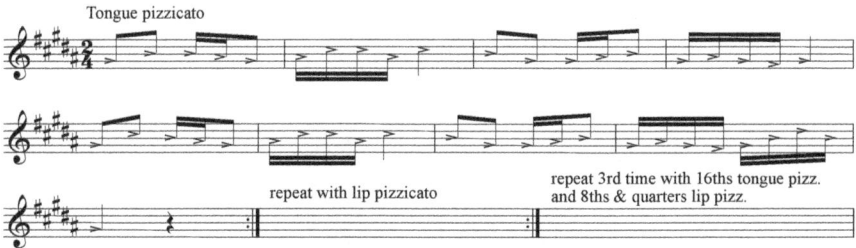

Figure 27e: Jennifer Borkowski, *Periodized Daily Studies Example*

Figure 27f: Jennifer Borkowski, *Periodized Daily Studies Example*

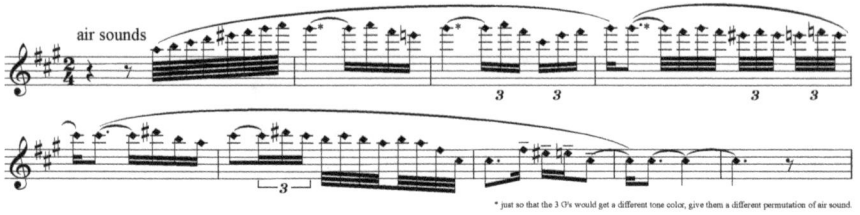

* just so that the 3 G's would get a different tone color, give them a different permutation of air sound.

Figure 27g: Jennifer Borkowski, *Periodized Daily Studies Example*

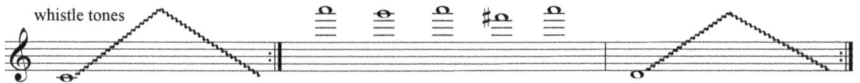

Figure 27h: Jennifer Borkowski, *Periodized Daily Studies Example*

Think of this as a structured workout. You are neither practicing at a constant level nor only increasing energy when you feel ready. You are working on your ability to call upon your energy when it is required. You are also working on your ability to immediately settle down. Use this model in other repertoire in your practice. Use the high energy techniques to wake yourself up and the low energy techniques to slow down and center. Experiment with repertoire right after the jet whistle. Then contrast this and experiment with repertoire right after whistle tones. Experiment with repertoire after any variances you feel in your energy level. Listen to differences in tone, resonance, phrasing and emotion that these techniques open in you.

IX. In Conclusion

New music is a special place. We're defining it as we go. We get our creative juices flowing. We are energized with new thoughts. Paradigm shifts in performance and pedagogical approach make us more complete musicians. The more approaches we have, the more depth we create and the more autonomous we become. In the suffering arts climate, these are invaluable skills.

Periodization does not need to takeover pedagogy as we know it, but its example can serve as an agent for increasing pedagogical depth. I've taken a few words: conscious, body-conscious, depth, strength, stamina, mind-set, and given them structure.

The fire and commitment of top athletes is something I've wanted to understand more deeply. I was inspired through my knowledge of periodization training and peak performance. The concept of periodization involves preparing the body in ways that musicians traditionally neglect. The concept of tapering work before a performance is something novel to many of us. Stamina building has been only guessed at to this point. The solutions here are solid as they are based on a tried and proven theory in sport science. Introducing these concepts gives us clear ways to physically prepare without adding to our stress levels. Periodization seeks to minimize injury and allow the body to peak at the right moments. The theory, when well applied, will lessen worry about preparedness and allow for more creativity and enjoyment during performances.

I've talked about developments in technology that change the game for us. I'm not at all for moving us backwards. I hope that my approach shows that we can integrate the newness while keeping the fire and work ethic in order to initiate the change that our forerunners underwent. There are more video tutorials appearing all the time. Use one, then another, then another. Don't stop at the basics. If someone's video helps you, send her a message and let her know. If you find someone else's more helpful, please don't compare. We're not building a pyramid on which we will one day place the crowned royalty of extended techniques. Extended techniques are about moving on. Look around. Composers are finding new paths. We do this a disservice when we approach them with a competitive mindset.

My hope is that this book also starts to deepen pedagogical discourse. Pedagogy is not only a skill and an art, but also a field of scholarship. When teaching professional and pre-professional musicians, the goal is to empower their autonomy and their decision-making integrity. The interdisciplinary nature of this opens doors for more questions.

Above all, we see that diving into a new score ultimately means a deeper connection with that score and the composer who wrote it. As was said earlier, through this work, I strengthen myself.

X. Bibliography

Abel, J. L., & Larkin, K. T. (1990). Anticipation of performance among musicians: Physiological arousal, confidence, and state-anxiety. *Psychology of Music, 18*(2), 171-182. doi: 10.1177/0305735690182006

Adolphe, B. (1991). *The mind's ear: Exercises for improving the musical imagination of performers, listeners, and composers.* St. Louis, MO: MMB Music.

Adolphe, B. (1996). *What to listen for in the world.* New York, NY: Limelight Editions.

Adorno, T. W., Leppert, R. D., & Gillespie, S. H. (2002). *Essays on music.* Berkeley, CA: University of California Press.

Allen, S. (2002). Teaching large ensemble music improvisation. *Radical Pedagogy.*

Anaerobic exercise: Energy without oxygen. (n.d.). *University of Iowa Healthcare.* Retrieved February 20, 2008, from http://www.uihealthcare.com/topics/exercisefitness/exer3098.html

Anderson, O. (n.d.). Periodization training. *Periodization Training Provides Athletes with a Varied and Progressive Routine.* Retrieved February 25, 2008, from http://www.pponline.co.uk/encyc/periodization-training-provides-athletes-with-a-varied-and-progressive-routine-645

Andraud (Ed.). (1941). *The modern flutist.* San Antonio, TX: Southern Music.

Artaud, P. Y. (1991). *Die Flöte.* Frankfurt am Main: Musikverlag Zimmerman.

Barta, A. G. (1998). Sources of information on woodwind multiphonics: An annotated bibliography. *Perspectives of New Music, 26*(1), 246-256.

Bartolozzi, B., & Mencarelli, P. L. (1973). *Nuova tecnica per strumento a fiato di legno.* Milano: Edizioni Suvini Zerboni.

Berio, L. (1958). *Sequenza per flauto solo.* Milano: Edizioni Suvini Zerboni.

Bledsoe, H. (n.d.). *Helen Bledsoe, Flutist.* Retrieved April 16, 2008, from http://www.helenbledsoe.com/

Bompa, T. O., & Calcina, O. (1994). *Theory and methodology of training: The key to athletic performance.* Dubuque, IA: Kendall/Hunt Pub.

Bompa, T. O. (1999). *Periodization: Theory and methodology of training.* Champaign, IL: Human Kinetics.

Borkowski, J. (2010, December). Integrating extended techniques into all levels of repertoire. *Flute Talk,* 8-10.

Borkowski, J. (2011). Fit to play: The fitness effect on physically challenging flute repertoire. *Medical Problems of Performing Artists, 26*(1), 63-64.

Borkowski, J. A. (2008). *From simple to complex: Extended techniques in flute literature; Incentive to integrate cognitive and kinesthetic awareness in university programs* (Unpublished doctoral dissertation). Universität für Musik und darstellende Kunst, Graz.

Boros, J. (1994). Why complexity? *Perspectives of New Music, 31*(1), 90-101.

Botros, A. (n.d.). *The virtual flute – Flute fingerings, alternate fingerings and multiphonic fingerings.* Retrieved June 27, 2013, from http://www.phys.unsw.edu.au/music/flute/virtual/main.html

Boutellier, U., Buchel, R., Kundert, A., & Spengler, C. (n.d.). *Research studies for athletes and COPD patients.* Retrieved February 25, 2008, from http://www.expand-a lung. com/Research_Studies/research_studies.html

Brandfonbrener, A. G. (1990). The epidemiology and prevention of hand and wrist injuries in performing artists. *Hand Clinics, 6*(3), 365-370.

Cage, J. (1961). *Silence: Lectures and writings.* Middletown, CT: Wesleyan University Press.

Chase, G. (1967). Review: New sources for new music. *Anuario, 3*(1), 77-84.

Christensen, T. S. (2002). *The Cambridge history of western music theory.* Cambridge: Cambridge University Press.

Chu, D. A. (1998). *Jumping into plyometrics.* Champaign, IL.: Human Kinetics.

Conditioning: Aerobic and anaerobic. (n.d.). *Welcome to U.S. Figure Skating.* Retrieved February 25, 2008, from http://www.usfigureskating.org/content/Conditioning Aerobic Anaerobic Nov Jun Snr.pdf.

Davids, K., Bennett, S., & Newell, K. M. (2006). *Movement system variability.* Champaign, IL: Human Kinetics.

Davies, H. (n.d.). Microtonality. *Home Page in Grove Music.* Retrieved February 25, 2008, from http://www.grovemusic.com/

Deleuze, G., & Guattari, F. (1987). *A thousand plateaus: Capitalism and schizophrenia.* Minneapolis, MN: University of Minnesota Press.

Deschenes, B. (1998). Toward an anthropology of music listening. *International Review of the Aesthetics and Sociology of Music, 29*(2), 135-153.

Dick, R. (1986). *Tone development through extended techniques.* New York, NY: Multiple Breath Music.

Dick, R. (1987). *Circular breathing for the flutist.* New York, NY: Multiple Breath Music.

Dick, R. (1987). *Flying lessons* (Vol. 1). St. Louis, MO: MMB Publishing.

Dick, R. (1989). *The other flute: A performance manual of contemporary techniques.* St. Louis, MO: MMB Music.

Dick, R. (2004, November 15). [E-mail to the author].

Dick, R. (n.d.). *Robert Dick - Modern Flutist.* Retrieved June 27, 2013, from http://www.robertdick.net/

Dürichen, C., & Kratsch, S. (Eds.). (n.d.). *Orchester Probespiel Flöte Piccolo* (EP 8659 ed.). Frankfurt am Main: Peters.

Ferneyhough, B., & Boros, J. (1990). Shattering the vessels of received wisdom. *Perspectives of New Music, 28*(2), 6-50.

Ferneyhough, B. (1975). *Cassandra's dream song, flute alone.* London: Peters Edition.

Ferneyhough, B. (1982). *Superscriptio: Solo piccolo.* London: Peters Edition.

Ferneyhough, B. (1993). Form-figure-style: An intermediate assessment. *Perspectives of New Music, 31*(1), 33-34.

Ferneyhough, B. (1993). The tactility of time. *Perspectives of New Music, 31*(1), 20-30.

Ferneyhough, B. (1994). Composing a viable (if transatory) self. *Perspectives of New Music, 32*(1), 32-40.

Fonville, J. (1991). Ben Johnston's extended just intonation: A guide for interpreters. *Perspectives of New Music, 29*(2), 106-137.

Frankel, C., & Kravitz, L., Ph.D. (n.d.). *Periodization.* Retrieved February 25, 2008, from http://www.unm.edu/~lkravitz/Article folder/periodization.html

Fry, H. J. (1984). Occupational maladies of musicians: Their cause and prevention. *International Journal of Music Education, 4*(1), 59-63. doi: 10.1177/025576148400400113

Furrer, B. (2001). *Auf tönernen füssen.* Kassel: Bärenreiter.

Gilmore, B. (2001). *Reconstructing Harry: Some current issues in the Partch biography, part 1.* Retrieved July 5, 2013, from http://www.corporeal.com/reconhp1.html

Glasgow, G. W. (1985). Quodlibet. *Perspectives of New Music, 24*(1), 330-335.

Guck, M. (1984). A flow of energy: Density 21.5. *Perspectives of New Music, 23*(1), 334-347.

Harby, K. (n.d.). *Larry Krantz flute pages: Beta blockers/performance anxiety.* Retrieved February 25, 2008, from http://www.larrykrantz.com/perfanx.htm

Harmat, L., & Theorell, T. (2010). Heart rate variability during singing and flute playing. *Music and Medicine, 2*(1), 10-17. doi: 10.1177/1943862109354598

Heiss, J. (1968). Some multiple-sonorities for flute, oboe, clarinet, and bassoon. *Perspectives of New Music, 7*(1), 136-142.

Heiss, J. (1972). The flute: New sounds. *Perspectives of New Music, 10*(2), 153-158.

Hertzog, C., Kramer, A. F., Wilson, R. S., & Lindenberger, U. (2008). Enrichment effects on adult cognitive development: Can the functional capacity of older adults be preserved and enhanced? *Psychological Science in the Public Interest, 9*(1), 1-65. doi: 10.1111/j.1539-6053.2009.01034.x

Holliger, H. (1988). *(t)air(e).* Mainz: Ars Viva Verlag.

Hosokawa, T. (1997). *Vertical Song I.* Japan: Schott.

Huber, K. (1980). *Ein Hauch von Unzeit.* Wiesbaden: Breitkopf & Härtl.

Ibert, J. (1934). *Concerto for Flute.* Paris: Alphonse Leduc.

The Kingma system flute. (n.d.). Retrieved November 15, 2004, from http://www.brannenflutes.com/kingma.html

Korde, S. (1991). *Tenderness of Cranes.* Acton, MA: Neuma.

Lachenmann, H., & Häusler, J. (1996). *Musik als existentielle Erfahrung: Schriften 1966-1995.* Wiesbaden: Breitkopf & Härtel.

Lahme, A. (2000). Current developments in music medicine. *International Journal of Music Education, 35*(1), 40-45. doi: 10.1177/025576140003500113

Lang, B. (2003). *Schrift I.* Wien: Zeitvertreib Verlag.

Lehmann, A. C., Sloboda, J. A., & Woody, R. H. (2007). *Psychology for musicians: Understanding and acquiring the skills.* Oxford: Oxford University Press.

Lehrer, P. M. (1987). A review of the approaches to the management of tension and stage fright in music performance. *Journal of Research in Music Education, 35*(3), 143. doi: 10.2307/3344957

Lemaître, F., Bernier, F., Petit, I., Renard, N., Gardette, B., & Joulia, F. (2005). Heart rate responses during a breath-holding competition in well-trained divers. *International Journal of Sports Medicine, 26*(6), 409-413. doi: 10.1055/s-2004-821159

Levi, L. (1964). The urinary output of adrenaline and noradrenaline during different experimentally induced pleasant and unpleasant emotional states: A summary. *Journal of Psychosomatic Research, 8*(3), 197-198. doi: 10.1016/0022-3999(64)90041-8

Levine, C., & Mitropoulos-Bott, C. (2004). *The techniques of flute playing. Die Spieltechnik der Flöte.* Kassel: Bärenreiter.

Levine, C. (2008, April 16). [E-mail to the author].

Louke, P. (n.d.). *Extended techniques.* Retrieved June 28, 2013, from http://palouke.home.comcast.net/~palouke/RepExtendedTechniques.htm

Magill, R. A. (2007). *Motor learning and control: Concepts and applications.* Boston, MA: McGraw-Hill.

Mason, M. K. (n.d.). *Theodor Adorno's theory of music and its social implications.* Retrieved June 28, 2013, from http://www.moyak.com/researcher/resume/papers/var9mkm.html

McLaren, B. (1998). A brief history of microtonality in the twentieth century. *Xenharmonikon, 17,* 57-110.

Measuring lung capacity. (n.d.). Retrieved June 28, 2013, from http://www.biology-corner.com/worksheets/lungcapacity.html

Messiaen, O. (1952). *Le merle noir, flute & piano.* Paris: Alphonse Leduc.

Microtonal Listening List. (n.d.). Retrieved June 28, 2013, from http://xenharmonic.wikispaces.com/MicrotonalListeningList

Möllendorff, W. (1917). *Musik mit Vierteltönen; Erfahrungen am bichromatischen Harmonium.* Leipzig: F.E.C. Leuckart.

Modern Flute / Piccolo / Alto Flute. (n.d.). Retrieved February 25, 2008, from http://www.fluteinfo.com/Fingering_chart/modern.php

Morgan, R. P. (1991). *Twentieth-century music: A history of musical style in modern Europe and America.* New York: Norton.

Mornell, A. (2002). *Lampenfieber und Angst bei ausübenden Musikern: Kritische Übersicht über die Forschung.* Frankfurt am Main: P. Lang.

Muller, T. (1997). 'Music is not a solitary act': Conversation with Luciano Berio. *Tempo,* (199), 16-20. doi: 10.1017/S0040298200005556

Nassar, L., Albano, J., & Padron, D. (1999). Exertional headache in a collegiate gymnast. *Clinical Journal of Sport Medicine, 9*(3), 182-183. doi: 10.1097/00042752-199907000-00013

Nicolet, A., & Reidemeister, P. (1974). *Pro musica nova: Studien zum spielen neuer Musik für Flöte: Studies for playing avant-garde music for flute.* Köln: Musikverlag H. Gerig.

Noakes, T. (2003). *Lore of running.* Champaign, IL: Human Kinetics.

Noakes, T. D. (2008). Testing for maximum oxygen consumption has produced a brainless mode of human exercise performance [Abstract]. *British Journal of Sports Medicine.* doi: 10.1136/bjsm.2008.046821

Noakes, T. D. (2012). Fatigue is a brain-derived emotion that regulates the exercise behavior to ensure the protection of whole body homeostasis. *Frontiers in Physiology, 3*(82). doi: 10.3389/fphys.2012.00082

Offermans, W. (1992). *For the contemporary flutist: Twelve studies for the flute with explanations in the supplement = Für den zeitgenössischen Flötisten.* Frankfurt am Main: Zimmermann.

O'Neill, S. & McPherson, G. (2002). "Motivation". In R. Parncutt & G. E. McPherson (Eds.). *The science & psychology of music performance: Creative strategies for teaching and learning.* Oxford: Oxford University Press, pp. 31-46.

Palmer, P. (1999). Heinz Holliger at 60. *Tempo*, (208), 29-32.

Parncutt, R. (2007). Can researchers help artists? Music performance research for music students. *Music Performance Research, 1*(1), 1-25.

Pellerite, J. J. (1972). *A modern guide to fingerings for the flute.* Bloomington, IN: Zalo Publications.

Plowman, S. A., & Smith, D. L. (2013). *Exercise physiology for health, fitness, and performance* (pp. 308-411). Philadelphia, PA: Lippincott Williams & Wilkins.

[Preface]. (1947). In H. Partch (Author), *Genesis of a music.* WI: University of Wisconsin Press.

Provost-Craig, M., Poe, C., Lawson, E., & Pitsos, D. (n.d.). *Novice, junior, senior, office strength & jump/plyometric yearly training schedule.* Retrieved June 28, 2013, from http://www.usfsa.org/content/strengthschedule.pdf

Ram. (n.d.). Retrieved June 28, 2013, from http://dictionary.reference.com/browse/ram?s=t

Röbke, P. (1990). *Der Instrumentalschüler als Interpret, Musikalische Spielräume im Instrumentalunterrich.* Mainz: B. Schott's Söhne.

Röbke, P. (2000). *Vom Handwerk zur Kunst. Didktische Grundlagen des Instrumentalunterrichts.* Mainz: Schott Musik International.

Rees, C. (n.d.). *Carla Rees – Alto and bass flute.* Retrieved June 28, 2013, from http://www.carlarees.co.uk/

Salmon, P., & Meyer, R. G. (1992). *Notes from the green room: Coping with stress and anxiety in musical performance.* New York, NY: Lexington Books.

Sample one year periodization schedule. (n.d.). *US Figure Skating.* Retrieved June 28, 2013, from http://www.usfigureskating.org/content/PeriodizationSchedule.pdf

Scheck, G. (1981). *Die Flöte und ihre Musik.* Leipzig: Deutsche Verlag für Musik.

Schick, S. (1994). Developing an interpretive context: Learning Brian Ferneyhough's Bone Alphabet. *Perspectives of New Music, 31*(1), 132-153.

Schiff, D. (1983). *The music of Elliott Carter.* London: Eulenburg Books.

Schopenhauer, A., & Hollingdale, R. J. (1970). *Essays and aphorisms.* Harmondsworth, Eng.: Penguin Books

Schott music – Harry Partch – Profil. (n.d.). Retrieved June 28, 2013, from http://www.schott-musik.de/shop/artists/1/38574/

Schulter, M. (n.d.). *What is microtonality.* Retrieved February 25, 2008, from http://members.tripod.com/~tuning_archive/on_site_tree/margoschulter/what_is_microtonality.html

Schwarzenbach, P., & Bryner-Kronjäger, B. (2005). *Üben ist doof. Gedanken und Anregungen für den Instrumentalunterricht.* Frauenfeld: Waldgut.

Schwindt-Gross, N. (1992). *Musikwissenschaftliches Arbeiten: Hilfsmittel, Techniken, Aufgaben* (5th ed.). Kassel: Bärenreiter.

Sciarrino, S. (1977). *L'opera per flauto*. Milano: Ricordi.

Selye, H. (1952). *The story of the adaptation syndrome, told in the form of informal, illustrated lectures*. Montreal: Acta.

Selye, H. (1974). *Stress without distress*. Philadelphia, PA: Lippincott.

Selye, H. (1978). *The stress of life*. New York, NY: McGraw-Hill.

Shapiro, J. (2005). Still searching for lost time. *Film Philosophy Journal, 9*(39).

Sherry, F. (2002). Never standing still. *Contemporary Music Review, 21*(1), 87-95. doi: 10.1080/07494460216639

Starer, R. (1969). *Rhythmic training*. New York, NY: MCA Music.

Stravinsky, I. (1985). *Firebird suite*. New York, NY: E. F. Kalmus.

Thompson, V. (1981). *A Virgil Thompson reader*. Boston, MA: Houghton Mifflin.

Trongone, J. A. (1948). Breath control for horn players. *Music Educators Journal, 34*(4), 40. doi: 10.2307/3387257

Vehrs, P. (1998). Prediction of VO2 max before, during, and after 16 weeks of endurance training. (maximal oxygen uptake). *Research Quarterly for Exercise and Sport.*

Volpi, F., & Sheehan, T. (1988). Hermeneia and Apophansis, the early Heidegger on Aristotle. In *Heidegger et l'idée de la phénoménologie* (pp. 67-80). Dordrecht: Kluwer Academic.

Wagner, A. (2004). Zeitgenossische Musik an Hochschulen. *Neue Zeitschrift Für Musik,* 16-17.

Waterman, E. (1994). Cassandra's dream song, A literary feminist perspective. *Perspectives of New Music, 32*(2), 154-172.

Wessel, H. (2001). D-transposition of the great arteries: Post-operative evaluation by breath-by-breath analysis of ventilation and pulmonary gas exchange during exercise. *European Heart Journal, 22*(12), 987-989. doi: 10.1053/euhj.2000.2572

Whittal, A. (1999). Holliger at 60, Keeping the Faith. *The Musical Times,* 38-48.

Wilmore, J. H., & Costill, D. L. (2004). *Physiology of sport and exercise*. Champaign, IL.: Human Kinetics.

Wolfe, J. (n.d.). *Flute Acoustics*. Retrieved June 28, 2013, from http://www.phys.unsw.edu.au/music/flute/

Wright, P. (2003, February). *American mavericks: Harry Partch's world*. Retrieved June 28, 2013, from http://musicmavericks.publicradio.org/features/essay_partchworld.html

Wright, P. (2003, February). *American Mavericks: Just Intonation*. Retrieved June 28, 2013, from http://musicmavericks.publicradio.org/features/essay_justintonation.html

Wulf, G., & Mornell, A. (2008). Insights about practice from the perspective of motor learning: A review. *Music Performance Research, 2,* 1-25.

Zender, H. (2004). *Die Sinne Denken, Texte zur Musik* (J. Hiekel, Ed.). Wiesbaden: Breitkopf & Härtl.

Ziegler, M. (n.d.). *Matthias Ziegler - soundworlds*. Retrieved June 28, 2013, from http://www.matthias-ziegler.ch/english/klangwelten/index.html

XI. Literature Recommendations by Subject

a. Resources for Modern Flute Music and Extended Techniques

Andraud (Ed.). (1941). *The modern flutist.* San Antonio, TX: Southern Music.

Artaud, P. Y. (1991). *Die Flöte.* Frankfurt am Main: Musikverlag Zimmerman.

Barta, A. G. (1998). Sources of information on woodwind multiphonics: An annotated bibliography. *Perspectives of New Music, 26*(1), 246-256.

Bledsoe, H. (n.d.). *Helen Bledsoe, Flutist.* Retrieved April 16, 2008, from http://www.helenbledsoe.com/

Borkowski, J. (2010, December). Integrating extended techniques into all levels of repertoire. *Flute Talk,* 8-10.

Borkowski, J. (2011). Fit to play: The fitness effect on physically challenging flute repertoire. *Medical Problems of Performing Artists, 26*(1), 63-64.

Borkowski, J. A. (2008). *From simple to complex: Extended techniques in flute literature; Incentive to integrate cognitive and kinesthetic awareness in university programs* (Unpublished doctoral dissertation). Universität für Musik und darstellende Kunst, Graz.

Botros, A. (n.d.). *The virtual flute - Flute fingerings, alternate fingerings and multiphonic fingerings.* Retrieved June 27, 2013, from http://www.phys.unsw.edu.au/music/flute/virtual/main.html

Dick, R. (1986). *Tone development through extended techniques.* New York, NY: Multiple Breath Music.

Dick, R. (1987). *Circular breathing for the flutist.* New York, NY: Multiple Breath Music.

Dick, R. (1987). *Flying lessons* (Vol. 1). St. Louis, MO: MMB Publishing.

Dick, R. (1989). *The other flute: A performance manual of contemporary techniques.* St. Louis, MO: MMB Music.

Dick, R. (n.d.). *Robert Dick - Modern Flutist.* Retrieved June 27, 2013, from http://www.robertdick.net/

Fonville, J. (1991). Ben Johnston's extended just intonation: A guide for interpreters. *Perspectives of New Music, 29*(2), 106-137.

Heiss, J. (1968). Some multiple-sonorities for flute, oboe, clarinet, and bassoon. *Perspectives of New Music, 7*(1), 136-142.

Heiss, J. (1972). The flute: New sounds. *Perspectives of New Music, 10*(2), 153-158.

Levine, C., & Mitropoulos-Bott, C. (2004). *The techniques of flute playing. Die Spieltechnik der Flöte.* Kassel: Bärenreiter.

Nicolet, A., & Reidemeister, P. (1974). *Pro musica nova: Studien zum spielen neuer Musik für Flöte: Studies for playing avant-garde music for flute.* Köln: Musikverlag H. Gerig.

Offermans, W. (1992). *For the contemporary flutist: Twelve studies for the flute with explanations in the supplement = Für den zeitgenössischen Flötisten.* Frankfurt am Main: Zimmermann.

Phyllis Louke - Extended techniques. (n.d.). Retrieved June 28, 2013, from http://palouke.home.comcast.net/~palouke/RepExtendedTechniques.htm

Rees, C. (n.d.). *Carla Rees - Alto and bass flute.* Retrieved June 28, 2013, from http://www.carlarees.co.uk/

Scheck, G. (1981). *Die Flöte und ihre Musik.* Leipzig: Deutsche Verlag für Musik.

Waterman, E. (1994). Cassandra's dream song, A literary feminist perspective. *Perspectives of New Music, 32*(2), 154-172.

Wolfe, J. (n.d.). *Flute Acoustics.* Retrieved June 28, 2013, from http://www.phys.unsw.edu.au/music/flute/

Ziegler, M. (n.d.). *Matthias Ziegler - soundworlds.* Retrieved June 28, 2013, from http://www.matthias-ziegler.ch/english/klangwelten/index.htm

b. Resources on Microtonality

Bartolozzi, B., & Mencarelli, P. L. (1973). *Nuova tecnica per strumento a fiato di legno.* Milano: Edizioni Suvini Zerboni.

Christensen, T. S. (2002). *The Cambridge history of western music theory.* Cambridge: Cambridge University Press.

Davies, H. (n.d.). Microtonality. *Home Page in Grove Music.* Retrieved February 25, 2008, from http://www.grovemusic.com/

Fonville, J. (1991). Ben Johnston's extended just intonation: A guide for interpreters. *Perspectives of New Music, 29*(2), 106-137.

McLaren, B. (1998). A brief history of microtonality in the twentieth century. *Xenharmonikon, 17,* 57-110.

Microtonal Listening List. (n.d.). Retrieved June 28, 2013, from http://xenharmonic.wikispaces.com/MicrotonalListeningList

Möllendorff, W. (1917). *Musik mit Vierteltönen; Erfahrungen am bichromatischen Harmonium.* Leipzig: F.E.C. Leuckart.

Schulter, M. (n.d.). *What is microtonality.* Retrieved February 25, 2008, from http://members.tripod.com/~tuning_archive/on_site_tree/margoschulter/what_is_microtonality.html

Wright, P. (2003, February). *American Mavericks: Just Intonation.* Retrieved June 28, 2013, from http://musicmavericks.publicradio.org/features/essay_justintonation.html

c. Resources on Music Pedagogy and Performance Research

Abel, J. L., & Larkin, K. T. (1990). Anticipation of performance among musicians: Physiological arousal, confidence, and state-anxiety. *Psychology of Music, 18*(2), 171-182. doi: 10.1177/0305735690182006

Adolphe, B. (1991). *The mind's ear: Exercises for improving the musical imagination of performers, listeners, and composers.* St. Louis, MO: MMB Music.

Adolphe, B. (1996). *What to listen for in the world.* New York, NY: Limelight Editions.

Allen, S. (2002). Teaching large ensemble music improvisation. *Radical Pedagogy.*

Fry, H. J. (1984). Occupational maladies of musicians: Their cause and prevention. *International Journal of Music Education, 4*(1), 59-63. doi: 10.1177/025576148400400113

Lahme, A. (2000). Current developments in music medicine. *International Journal of Music Education, 35*(1), 40-45. doi: 10.1177/025576140003500113

Lehmann, A. C., Sloboda, J. A., & Woody, R. H. (2007). *Psychology for musicians: Understanding and acquiring the skills.* Oxford: Oxford University Press.

Lehrer, P. M. (1987). A review of the approaches to the management of tension and stage fright in music performance. *Journal of Research in Music Education, 35*(3), 143. doi: 10.2307/3344957

Lehrer, P. M. (1987). A review of the approaches to the management of tension and stage fright in music performance. *Journal of Research in Music Education, 35*(3), 143. doi: 10.2307/3344957

Mornell, A. (2002). *Lampenfieber und Angst bei ausübenden Musikern: Kritische Übersicht über die Forschung.* Frankfurt am Main: P. Lang.

Parncutt, R., & McPherson, G. (2002). *The science & psychology of music performance: Creative strategies for teaching and learning.* Oxford: Oxford University Press.

Parncutt, R. (2007). Can researchers help artists? Music performance research for music students. *Music Performance Research, 1*(1), 1-25.

Röbke, P. (1990). *Der Instrumentalschüler als Interpret, Musikalische Spielräume im Instrumentalunterrich.* Mainz: B. Schott's Söhne.

Röbke, P. (2000). *Vom Handwerk zur Kunst, Didktische Grundlagen des Instrumentalunterrichts.* Mainz: Schott Musik International.

Salmon, P., & Meyer, R. G. (1992). *Notes from the green room: Coping with stress and anxiety in musical performance.* New York, NY: Lexington Books.

Schick, S. (1994). Developing an interpretive context: Learning Brian Ferneyhough's Bone Alphabet. *Perspectives of New Music, 31*(1), 132-153.

Schwarzenbach, P., & Bryner-Kronjäger, B. (2005). *Üben ist doof. Gedanken und Anregungen für den Instrumentalunterricht.* Frauenfeld: Waldgut.

Wulf, G., & Mornell, A. (2008). Insights about practice from the perspective of motor learning: A review. *Music Performance Research, 2*, 1-25.

d. Resources on Periodization and Physical Conditioning

Anaerobic exercise: Energy without oxygen. (n.d.). *University of Iowa Healthcare.* Retrieved February 20, 2008, from http://www.uihealthcare.com/topics/exercisefitness/exer3098.html

Anderson, O. (n.d.). Periodization training. *Periodization Training Provides Athletes with a Varied and Progressive Routine.* Retrieved February 25, 2008, from http://www.pponline.co.uk/encyc/periodization-training-provides-athletes-with-a-varied-and-progressive-routine-645

Bompa, T. O., & Calcina, O. (1994). *Theory and methodology of training: The key to athletic performance.* Dubuque, IA: Kendall/Hunt Pub.

Bompa, T. O. (1999). *Periodization: Theory and methodology of training.* Champaign, IL: Human Kinetics.

Borkowski, J. (2011). Fit to play: The fitness effect on physically challenging flute repertoire. *Medical Problems of Performing Artists, 26*(1), 63-64.

Boutellier, U., Buchel, R., Kundert, A., & Spengler, C. (n.d.). *Research studies for athletes and COPD patients*. Retrieved February 25, 2008, from http://www.expand-a lung. com/Research_Studies/research_studies.html

Chu, D. A. (1998). *Jumping into plyometrics*. Champaign, IL.: Human Kinetics.

Conditioning: Aerobic and anaerobic. (n.d.). *Welcome to U.S. Figure Skating*. Retrieved February 25, 2008, from http://www.usfigureskating.org/content/Conditioning Aerobic Anaerobic Nov Jun Snr.pdf.

Davids, K., Bennett, S., & Newell, K. M. (2006). *Movement system variability*. Champaign, IL: Human Kinetics.

Frankel, C., & Kravitz, L., Ph.D. (n.d.). *Periodization*. Retrieved February 25, 2008, from http://www.unm.edu/~lkravitz/Article folder/periodization.html

Lemaître, F., Bernier, F., Petit, I., Renard, N., Gardette, B., & Joulia, F. (2005). Heart rate responses during a breath-holding competition in well-trained divers. *International Journal of Sports Medicine, 26*(6), 409-413. doi: 10.1055/s-2004-821159

Levi, L. (1964). The urinary output of adrenaline and noradrenaline during different experimentally induced pleasant and unpleasant emotional states: A summary. *Journal of Psychosomatic Research, 8*(3), 197-198. doi: 10.1016/0022-3999(64)90041-8

Measuring lung capacity. (n.d.). Retrieved June 28, 2013, from http://www.biology-corner.com/worksheets/lungcapacity.html

Nassar, L., Albano, J., & Padron, D. (1999). Exertional headache in a collegiate gymnast. *Clinical Journal of Sport Medicine, 9*(3), 182-183. doi: 10.1097/00042752-199907000-00013

Noakes, T. (2003). *Lore of running*. Champaign, IL: Human Kinetics.

Noakes, T. D. (2008). Testing for maximum oxygen consumption has produced a brainless mode of human exercise performance [Abstract]. *British Journal of Sports Medicine*. doi: 10.1136/bjsm.2008.046821

Noakes, T. D. (2012). Fatigue is a brain-derived emotion that regulates the exercise behavior to ensure the protection of whole body homeostasis. *Frontiers in Physiology, 3*(82). doi: 10.3389/fphys.2012.00082

Plowman, S. A., & Smith, D. L. (2013). *Exercise physiology for health, fitness, and performance* (pp. 308-411). Philadelphia, PA: Lippincott Williams & Wilkins.

Selye, H. (1952). *The story of the adaptation syndrome, told in the form of informal, illustrated lectures*. Montreal: Acta.

Selye, H. (1974). *Stress without distress*. Philadelphia, PA: Lippincott.

Selye, H. (1978). *The stress of life*. New York, NY: McGraw-Hill.

Trongone, J. A. (1948). Breath control for horn players. *Music Educators Journal, 34*(4), 40. doi: 10.2307/3387257

Vehrs, P. (1998). Prediction of VO2 max before, during, and after 16 weeks of endurance training. (maximal oxygen uptake). *Research Quarterly for Exercise and Sport*.

Wessel, H. (2001). D-transposition of the great arteries: Post-operative evaluation by breath-by-breath analysis of ventilation and pulmonary gas exchange during exercise. *European Heart Journal, 22*(12), 987-989. doi: 10.1053/euhj.2000.2572

Wilmore, J. H., & Costill, D. L. (2004). *Physiology of sport and exercise.* Champaign, IL.: Human Kinetics.

e. Resources on Music Theory and Aesthetics

Adorno, T. W., Leppert, R. D., & Gillespie, S. H. (2002). *Essays on music.* Berkeley, CA: University of California Press.
Boros, J. (1994). Why complexity? *Perspectives of New Music, 31*(1), 90-101.
Cage, J. (1961). *Silence: Lectures and writings.* Middletown, CT: Wesleyan University Press.
Chase, G. (1967). Review: New sources for new music. *Anuario, 3*(1), 77-84.
Deschenes, B. (1998). Toward an anthropology of music listening. *International Review of the Aesthetics and Sociology of Music, 29*(2), 135-153.
Ferneyhough, B., & Boros, J. (1990). Shattering the vessels of received wisdom. *Perspectives of New Music, 28*(2), 6-50.
Ferneyhough, B. (1993). Form-figure-style: An intermediate assessment. *Perspectives of New Music, 31*(1), 33-34.
Ferneyhough, B. (1993). The tactility of time. *Perspectives of New Music, 31*(1), 20-30.
Ferneyhough, B. (1994). Composing a viable (if transatory) self. *Perspectives of New Music, 32*(1), 32-40.
Lachenmann, H., & Häusler, J. (1996). *Musik als existentielle Erfahrung: Schriften 1966-1995.* Wiesbaden: Breitkopf & Härtel.
Mason, M. K. (n.d.). *Theodor Adorno's theory of music and its social implications.* Retrieved June 28, 2013, from http://www.moyak.com/researcher/resume/papers/var9mkm.html
Muller, T. (1997). 'Music is not a solitary act': Conversation with Luciano Berio. *Tempo, 3*(199), 16. doi: 10.1017/S0040298200005556
Palmer, P. (1999). Heinz Holliger at 60. *Tempo,* (208), 29-32.
[Preface]. (1947). In H. Partch (Author), *Genesis of a music.* WI: University of Wisconsin Press.
Schick, S. (1994). Developing an interpretive context: Learning Brian Ferneyhough's Bone Alphabet. *Perspectives of New Music, 31*(1), 132-153.
Shapiro, J. (2005). Still searching for lost time. *Film Philosophy Journal, 9*(39).
Sherry, F. (2002). Never standing still. *Contemporary Music Review, 21*(1), 87-95. doi: 10.1080/07494460216639
Waterman, E. (1994). Cassandra's dream song, A literary feminist perspective. *Perspectives of New Music, 32*(2), 154-172.
Wright, P. (2003, February). *American mavericks: Harry Partch's world.* Retrieved June 28, 2013, from http://musicmavericks.publicradio.org/features/essay_partchworld.html
Zender, H. (2004). *Die Sinne Denken, Texte zur Musik* (J. Hiekel, Ed.). Wiesbaden: Breitkopf & Härtl.

XII. Graded Repertoire List

Level 1

Louke, Phyllis, *Extended Techniques-Solos for Fun,* published by ALRY, 2006
Louke, Phyllis, *Extended Techniques-Double the Fun,* published by ALRY, 2003

Level 2

Erb, Donald, *Music for Mother Bear for Solo Alto Flute,* published Merion Music, Inc., 1970 (Can be played on the flute as well)
Folio, Cynthia, *Flute Fantasy,* published by the composer, 1976, Etudes and short concert pieces
Fortin, Viktor, *No Problem,* 14 easy duets with annotations and commentaries by Arno Steinwider-Johannsen, published by Döblinger, 2006
Gasser, Ulrich, *Papierblüten (Paper Blossoms),* published by Riccordi, 1982-84
Heiss, John, *Etudes for Solo Flute, Op. 20,* published by JBE and Son Music, 1986
Holland, Linda, *Easing into Extended Techniques,* published by Con Brio, 2000
Lorrain, Denis, *Du jour, la nuit,* published by Lemoine, 1995
Louke, Phyllis, *Extended Techniques-Solos for Fun,* published by ALRY, 2006
Louke, Phyllis, *Extended Techniques-Double the Fun,* published by ALRY, 2003
Offermans, Wil, *Für den jungen Flötisten (For the Young Flutist),* published by Zimmerman, 1995
Offermans, Will, *Für den Zeitgenössischen Flötistin (For the Contemporary Flutist),* published by Zimmerman, 1992, 12 Etudes, each focusing on one technique
Stahmer, Klaus Hinrich, *Aristofaniada for flute solo,* published by Zimmerman, 1979
Van Buren, John, *Incandescence,* published by Edition Modern
Veilhan, Francois, *Sonorite et techniques contemporaines (Sound and Contemporary Techniques for the flute),* published by Lemoine, 2006 Nine Etudes with exercises
Wye, Trevor, *A Very Easy 20th Century Album,* published by Novello, 1990

Level 3

Aitken, Robert, *Plainsong,* published by Universal Edition, 1977
Aitken, Robert, *Icicle,* published by Éditions Musicales Transatlantiques, 1977
Bennet, Richard Rodney, *Six Tunes for the Instruction of Singing Birds,* Published by Novello, 1962
Brown, Elizabeth, *Trillium,* published by Queztal, 1999
Corbett, Sid, *Cactus Flower,* published by Moeck, 1988
Dick, Robert, *Flying Lessons, Volume I,* published by MMB Music, 1987
Dick, Robert, *Flying Lessons, Volume II,* published by MMB Music, 1987
Dick, Robert, *Lookout,* published by MMB Music, 1989
Dick, Robert, *Tone Development Through Extended Techniques,* published by MMB Music, 1985

Dick, Robert, *Fish are Jumping,* published by MMB Music, 1999
Dick, Robert, *Or,* published by MMB Music, 1984
Folio, Cynthia, *Acra Sacra,* published by Hildegarde publishing, 1997
Fukushima, Kuzuo, *Mei,* published by Zerboni, 1962
Granados, Marco, *Le Bella y...and el Terco,* available from the NFA Library, 2007
Heiss, John, *Fantasia Appasionata, Episode IV,* available from the NFA Library, 1994
Higdon, Jennifer, *Song for Solo Flute,* available from the NFA Library, 1995
Huber, Nicolaus A., *First Play Mozart,* published by Breitkopf & Härtel, 1993
Kidde, Geoffrey, *Night Flight,* available from the NFA Library, 2002
La Berge, Anne, *Revamper,* published by Frog Peak Music, 1992
Martino, Donald, *Quodlibets I,* published by Dantalian, 1962
Martino, Donald, *Quodlibets II,* published by Dantalian, 1980
Messiaen, Olivier, *Le Merle, Noir,* published by Alphonse Leduc, 1951
Miserell-Mitchell, Janice, *Sometimes the City Is Silent,* available from the NFA Library, 2003
Payne, Maggie, *Reflections,* available from the NFA Library, 2004
Schocker, Gary, *Short Stories for Flute Alone,* published by Theodor Presser, 1999
Scelsi, Giacinto, *Quays,* published by Bärenreiter, 1953
Scelsi, Giacinto, *Pwyll,* published by Bärenreiter, 1954
Solum, John, *The American Flute,* published by MMB Music, 1994, A collection of short concert pieces
Yun, Isang, *Sori,* published by Bote and Bock, 1988
Ziegler, Matthias, *Morceau de Concours,* published by Mathias Ziegler, 2004

Level 4

Berio, Luciano, *Sequenza I,* published by Universal Editions, 1958
Carter, Elliot, *Scrivo in Vento,* published by Boosey and Hawkes, 1991
Furrer, Beat, *auf tönernen füssen,* published by Bärenreiter, 2001
Furrer, Beat, *Presto,* published by Bärenreiter, 1997
Holliger, Heinz, *Sonate (in)solit(air)e,* published by Scott, 1988
Hosokawa, Toshio, *Atem Lied,* published by Scott Japan, 1997
Hosokawa, Toshio, *Vertical Song I,* published by Scott Japan, 1997
Korde, Shirish, *Tenderness of Cranes,* published by Neuma Publishing, 1991
Nicolet, Aurele, *Pro Musica Nova / Studies for Playing Avant-Garde Music,* published by Breitkopf & Härtel, 1974
Offermans, Will, *Nesting Cranes,* published by Zimmermann, 1999
Stockhausen, Karl-Heinz, *In Freundschaft,* published by Stockhausen Verlag, 1977
Takemitsu, Toru, *Itinerant,* published by Schott, 1989
Takemitsu, Toru, *Voice,* published by Schott, 1971
Zender, Hans, *Lo-Shu II,* published by Bote and Bock, 1978

Level 5

Boulez, Pierre, *Sonatine for Flute and Piano*, published by amphion, 1946
Dick, Robert, *Afterlight*, published by MMB Music, 1973
Dillon James, *Sgothan*, published by C.F. Peters, 1984
Ferneyhough, Brian, *Cassandra's Dream Song*, published by Peters, 1970
Ferneyhough, Brian, *Superscripto for Piccolo*, published by Peters, 1981
Ferneyhough, Brian, *Unity Capsule*, for Bass Flute published by Peters, 1975-76
Haas, Georg Friedrich, *Finale*, published by Universal Edition, 2005
Holliger, Heinz, *Lied*, published by Breitkopf & Härtl, 1971
Holliger, Heinz, *(t)air(e)*, published by European American, 1980-83
Kawashima, Motoharu, *Manic Psychosis*, published by Japan Composers Society, 1991-92
Lang, Bernhard, *Schrift I*, published by Zeitvertreib Wien Berlin, 2003
Sciarrino, Salvatore, *L,opera per flauto, published by Riccordi*, 1977

THE ART AND SCIENCE OF MUSIC TEACHING AND PERFORMANCE

Series Editor Adina Mornell

www.peterlang.com

www.ingramcontent.com/pod-product-compliance
Lightning Source LLC
Chambersburg PA
CBHW020349100426
42812CB00001B/4